FINDING THE SONG:

Living After Attempting

Suicide

Amy R. Saltz

FINDING THE SONG:

Living After Attempting Suicide

Copyright © 2020 by Amy R. Saltz

Independently Published through KDP

Cover artwork by Mike T. Cherry

www.livingafterattemptingsuicide.com

ISBN: 978-1698963969

Dedicated to those who have

considered or attempted suicide

and to my soulmates

PART ONE

1

"Starless"

by

King Crimson

So, you want to know how I was able to find the song (to live a full and meaningful life) after being maimed by a suicide attempt? I've been asking myself the same question. Do you have some time? Let's hang out together for a while, and I'll try to answer both of us.

Music has always been my one consistent link to life and my truest vehicle for the flow of emotions. It offers me an outlet to express certain feelings that are extremely uncomfortable (such as anger, for example). Whether it be the lyrics, voices, instruments, tune, or a combination of these, certain songs connect with me so deeply that they can embody an emotional experience. For each chapter, I'll mention a song to you with its artist, and you can search online for it. Finding the song can help guide us.

I believe that what's happening inside the self—the inner state of being (possibly, but not always, in response to what's happening around the person)—is what causes an individual to consider suicide. It's how I was feeling internally that caused me to want/need to die. I choose to refrain from sharing details of the external events that contributed to my suicidality. The suffering is what matters—and it's valid no matter what.

As an adult, I hold firmly to the belief that we can recover emotionally from just about anything if we're treated with compassion and given validation. As a youth in my early teens, I reached out for help. For reasons unknown to me, I was repeatedly invalidated. The invalidation caused my emotional pain to intensify and become accompanied by deep shame.

There was an enveloping darkness inside me that wouldn't go away. It inhabited my mind and my spirit. It was worsening every day. I felt alone and disconnected from the world around me, analogous to an astronaut whose lifeline has been severed and is dangling in the dark void of space.

Music was the only entity I felt I could access, and I isolated myself within its cavernous passages. It took me away from the outside world. I could see life going on around me, but I couldn't find a way to be included in it. Joy and meaning were strangers to me. At birthday time, when making a wish before blowing out the candles on the cake, I'd wish that I could be happy one day. I was functioning, but without hope. I was a lost teen holding onto nothingness.

It's hard to fathom, but during this time I was the number 1 student in my class. Perfect scores were what I had to obtain in order to camouflage my lack of self-esteem. If there was an extra credit for 4 points (so the total could be 104) and I got only 100, I'd obsess all day and night over how I missed that one question.

I'd put a great deal of pressure upon myself, and it was adding to my downfall. You see, as a child I had encephalitis from chicken pox. I'd been quarantined and missed most of the first grade. When I was finally released, no one checked for any brain complications. I noticed in second grade that something was different with my ability to read. Somehow the words were washed away as I read them, like when the ocean's waves wash away writing in the sand. This condition never got better. I could sound out and read the words aloud perfectly so was always placed in accelerated classes, but comprehension was lacking. I'd write everything down in notebooks and memorize it so I could score well on tests. When it came time to read whole books, though, I was in big trouble.

No one seemed to think anything was wrong with me because of my high marks. I was allowed to take psychology as an incoming junior when it was on the roster for seniors only. On "Career Day" it was decided that my "career path" was to become a psychologist, and that I should consider Harvard when it was time to apply to colleges. The pressure to continue performing at this level felt unsustainable, and I was very worried about taking the Scholastic Aptitude Test. I feared I'd be exposed like the wizard behind the curtain in Oz. This concern, on top of other experiences that felt overwhelming to me, may have toppled me over. It pushed me to feel as though I had to "get out of Dodge."

As an adult, I got tested at a prestigious hospital and was asked by the sympathetic reading specialist if I'd ever had encephalitis—because, she explained, the neurological testing indicates that I have a serious, incurable disability from it. I share this with you now because it's quite a challenge for me to read what I write! My previous book was a perfect length for me to proofread—32 pages including illustrations. That book was a metaphorical story. This book is nonfiction.

2

"Errors of My Way"

by

Wishbone Ash

Even though it's brutal for me to tell you the details of the suicide attempt, it's necessary to do so to put us at the starting point of how to live afterwards. Bear with me. Please don't leave me while I share this. I promise to take us away from the abyss once it has been delineated.

Feelings of sorrow and anguish had become unbearable. I desperately sought healing, but it wasn't there for me. Instead, I was significantly harmed by a therapist in the process of seeking help, and I had to continue going back there even though trust had been broken. After the worst session, I was dropped off at Hebrew school as if nothing had happened. Simultaneously, when in junior high, a married teacher of mine confided in me that he'd fallen in love with me. While the attention was captivating, what he wanted was way over my head. I didn't feel safe in the world or with myself.

By the time I got to high school, all of my energy went towards getting straight A's without being able to read properly and holding myself together as my trust was being shattered. Something was very wrong with me, and I didn't understand it.

I'd just seen the movie *One Flew Over the Cuckoo's Nest*, and I imagined that perhaps I'd be safer in a mental institution. It could be a way to escape. I tried to hurt myself, and I was sent to a psychiatric hospital. Maybe in a hospital there'd be a chance to get help. Unfortunately, no matter how hard I tried to reach out for assistance, my experiences and feelings were invalidated. I was told that I didn't deserve to be in the hospital—that I shouldn't have any problems since I was the number 1 student.

A psychiatrist put me on a medication that lowered my blood pressure. When I got up the next morning, I blacked out and fell headfirst with my chin hitting the metal bed frame. Stitches were required, and bonding was necessary for the broken teeth. A nurse performed ECT (electroconvulsive therapy) on my roommate while I was in the room. It was horrifying to see, and the equipment blocked the doorway so I couldn't get out. It was not safe for me there. After several months, I was returned to the same set of circumstances I'd been enduring before—except now my classmates knew where I'd been.

I was undone. I couldn't stay this way for much longer. The next thing I knew, I was in another psychiatric hospital after trying to jump out the window of the high school. A teacher had caught me by the ankles and dragged me back inside. I was then transported to the hospital. Could I be helped this time? I begged for help. Lamentably, I was invalidated again. I was told that if I really wanted to die, I'd be dead by now. This was devastating to me. In addition, it was scary because life-threatening substances were accessible there. As unsafe as I felt, I was allowed to go outside by myself.

I found myself alone in the woods, petrified. I felt like I was having a breakdown. Inside of me there were two voices speaking: one was harsh and controlling, demanding that I do this; the other was soft and meek, begging me not to do it. I'm not sure where my own voice had gone. The cruel one won, and a container of Drano was opened and poured into my mouth. Excruciating pain gripped me (from the burning that occurs when the lye meets with saliva). I saw pieces of my face fall to the ground as I tried to spit out the poison.

I ran into the street hoping to get run over so the pain would cease. A driver swerved to avoid hitting me, and I was rushed into an ambulance—still burning all the way to another hospital. When I was wheeled in, a nurse held morphine over my head saying that she hated people like me; there were people with cancer, and I did this. Her contempt for me was palpable. She delayed giving me pain relief. Since I couldn't speak, I wrote on a pad of paper that

I was sorry. This spoke volumes about how I regarded myself.

The pain was indescribable. I was in the ICU hooked up to a ventilator and finally given morphine. When removed from the ventilator and fully conscious, all I wanted was a drink of water. There was a pitcher on the table, but I learned that I could no longer eat or drink by mouth. Without explanation, I was wheeled into the OR where I watched and spasmed in agony as my abdomen was cut open with only local anesthesia for insertion of a gastrostomy tube into which formula would be pumped by syringe. Concurrently, without any anesthesia, an endotracheal procedure was performed to maintain my airway. With the burns in that area, it was harrowing.

I was moved to a hospital room, then put in restraints and connected to multiple IVs. I must have been allergic to something because I developed dermatographia (itchy raised hives on the skin from any touching). The staff came in and played tic tac toe on my skin, laughing and having fun while I suffered. I couldn't speak and was buckled to bed rails while this happened. I didn't feel human. I felt hated.

At this point, I was in a state of shock. This may be what kept me alive. I had been experiencing deep emotional pain before; now it was accompanied by unimaginable physical pain and loss of basic functions and body parts. My mouth and lips were severely burned and swollen shut. Most of my tongue was burned away. What remained of it was stuck to the bottom of my mouth with no mobility. The pain and swelling from the burns made it impossible to talk. When the swelling subsided, I could try to speak, but the loss of most of my tongue and inability to open my mouth or move my lips to enunciate meant my words were most often not understood. Swallowing was quite difficult. To manage my saliva, I had to continually briskly suck in air, which made a disruptive sound. In order to eat, I had to put formula into a large syringe and pump it into the gastrostomy tube protruding from my stomach. Come to think of it, I was a real mess! I was 16 and 17 during this time, now I'm almost 60. The suicide attempt took only a few seconds, but it changed my life forever.

How are you holding up? Writing this for you gave me something I wasn't expecting. For the first time in four decades, I actually felt pure compassion for myself as opposed to blaming myself or feeling at fault. This suicide attempt was a tragedy. I'd been reaching out and trying to receive help. I was disintegrating until I completely broke apart. Doing this terrible thing seemed to bring my true inner voice back—even though I couldn't speak.

3

"Entangled"

by

Genesis

After many months of physiological hospitalization, I was sent on the next phase of my journey—put in another ambulance, this time to spend years in mental institutions. Some were like dungeons and had bars on the windows. These years stripped me of any prospects for dignity. I had to take formula and meds in my G-tube in front of the other patients. Some patients made fun of me. Pieces of my mouth were still falling off as the scarring from the burns tightened. I couldn't eat by mouth, and meals were the only activity patients looked forward to doing together. I couldn't participate, but had to watch as everyone ate. I had to smell the food I couldn't have. I got the sense from most of the staff that "I made my own bed, so I must now lie in it."—that the situation I was in was my own fault—that I was to blame for my actions. The message seemed to be that I was a bad person. Many of the patients were psychotic and some were violent. I saw one try to break a nurse's neck, and another set fire to the ward. The worst of life's tragedies were there—more than a 17-year-old could fathom

What made me stay alive there was fear...that if I tried to kill myself, I'd not succeed and would experience even more physical torture. In addition to fear, I was given a new hope. There'd be reconstructive surgery/skin grafts for the burns and scarring. I didn't get detailed info, so I thought the docs would put me back to the way I was before the incident. That kept me going.

The surgeries were quite painful with skin taken from around my upper thighs. My ass is literally in my mouth! There were multiple operations, back and forth from one hospital to the other. Before one of the operations, the surgeon took me to another girl's room. She was my age, but I was told she had a spinal cord injury that she didn't cause. I looked down hiding my tears, wanting to become invisible. The message seemed to be that some problems were worthy of compassion and some weren't. Mine fell into the latter category.

After various procedures, an uncomfortable prosthetic device had to be worn in my mouth to prevent the skin grafts from failing. Over time, the grafts adhered and there was improvement. My mouth was no longer burned shut and could now open somewhat (nowhere near the normal width). My lips were constructed from skin grafts. With such extensive oral scarring, my mouth wasn't anything like what it was before. The worst part was that the surgeons couldn't restore my tongue because it's a muscle. I never realized the vital importance of that body part.

During the time the prosthetic device was being worn, my class was graduating high school. I still had to eat via the gastrostomy tube and couldn't speak clearly. The prosthesis was similar to having a large, thick chunk of orange peel in my mouth but a lot harder in texture and a little lighter in color.

Between this and the scarring, I was a sight that made eyes sore!

The mental hospital offered to give me a pass to attend the graduation, and with trepidation I accepted. Even though my class rank was #1 (and I had to complete a course load while in the hospital), I was dismissed from being valedictorian. At the time, I was crushed. It was so incredibly challenging to be there in the state I was in and for my ranking to be overlooked. However, when my name was called, the entire class (even kids who'd been tough on me) and the audience got up to give me a standing ovation. Afterwards, the class celebrated their graduation while I was taken back to the mental hospital. As an adult, I'm proud of myself for rising to the occasion and feel quite moved by how the class rose too!

The hope I'd been holding onto disappeared when I faced the permanent extent of my injuries. This derailed me. Between enduring all the operations, struggling with impaired speech, and not finding compassion, I didn't have the chance to focus on underlying issues and to discuss my feelings. Not being able to eat by mouth felt like severe deprivation. I'd see food when I looked at people—a thin person was a banana, a stout person was a muffin, a muscular person was a loaf of bread. Each patient in the mental hospital was suffering in such an intense way; there wasn't much opportunity for connection. Sometimes terrible things happened to the patients or they did unspeakable things to others.

Time passed very slowly. Here was a typical day: get up (if able to sleep); watch everyone eat breakfast (wishing I could have some); have silverware counted by staff; stand in line for meds and formula to be pumped via syringe into my gastrostomy tube while patients gawk (double over in pain if formula is cold); sit on a chair that someone had peed on; hear the same Earth, Wind & Fire album playing over and over while a patient does ballet in a tutu, bathing cap, and flippers, while another bangs her head against the wall and gets a shot of Thorazine; watch everyone eat lunch (wishing I could have some); have silverware counted by staff; stand in line for meds and formula again; freak out when a button is pushed and big men come storming in to wrap someone up in cold packs; freak out again when someone is locked into seclusion; watch everyone eat supper (wishing I could have some); have silverware counted by staff; stand in line for meds and formula; pray I could lose my mind (but it kept staying with me)!

While my classmates were off to learn at university or at a job, I had to teach myself how to talk and eat. I was told that I might never be able to talk or eat by mouth and would likely be institutionalized for life. Once the prosthetic device was removed, I could speak in a somewhat less muffled, more intelligible manner. Eating by mouth was still not possible, but I was able to sip and swallow water. I tried putting pieces of food in my mouth, but they either fell out or got stuck. Then I had an idea. What if I chose soft, moist food and used a fork to maneuver it so it could be chewed and then drank lots of water to push it back to my throat so it could be swallowed? It worked! They still wanted me to keep the gastrostomy tube. I hated that thing. Sometimes it fell out and my guts leaked. Once they shoved it back in, and I got a potentially fatal infection. That's when they finally agreed to remove it.

4

"Pyramids"

by

Spooky Tooth

After not being able to eat by mouth for several years, I then couldn't stop! Sadly, I developed a formidable eating disorder. For some reason (probably related to the shame I'd been feeling), I couldn't allow myself to keep the food inside of me, but I needed enormous quantities. I'd throw it all up and then start again. As you might imagine, this was quite detrimental for my skin grafts as well as for the rest of my body. I lost quite a lot of weight. I had sores in my mouth and throat, seizures, an electrolyte imbalance, cardiovascular complications, and needed to be on IVs again. It was awful. I think I was addicted to food. Oh, I craved help! Here was another example of a problem that didn't seem to garner compassion.

After some inpatient treatment that felt particularly cruel, I wound up at a hospital with a program specifically for eating disorders. Finally, all the patients were viewed with care. It was so much more humane than the mental hospitals. I fully committed myself to recovering. I'd been longing for healing for such a long time. Could this be my chance? I earnestly followed the protocol. I learned what the proper amounts were and to eat those at mealtimes. I also learned how to find other ways to fill myself up.

Since I'd been hospitalized for so long, it was recommended that I go to live in a halfway house upon discharge to ensure a complete and permanent rehabilitation. Eating disorders are rough because you can't abstain from food, but I never binged and purged again. I researched the various halfway houses and chose one that seemed to be in a vibrant town as opposed to one right near the hospital. This choice led me to life!

The behavioral therapy helped cure my eating disorder, but the rest of me was still unhealed. Because of all that happened, there wasn't room for processing. Everything had to be digested without understanding. In this context, the eating disorder seems like a natural outcome.

Looking back, I see that even though the eating disorder could've killed me, it turned out to be a lifesaver. It gave me the opportunity to see that there were other forms of treatment, and that I had the strength and perseverance to come through. I realize now that I truly sought healing. It wasn't a choice to attempt suicide. Patients seem to be blamed and judged as if they had made a conscious choice with clear minds. This wasn't the case for me, and I don't think it is in general. Lack of clarity about this may be where some of the judgment that blocks compassion for those who have attempted suicide resides.

Going into the world after being hospitalized for so long was like being from another planet. I missed my late teens and early twenties and had to face being without most of my tongue and being with the resulting scarring and hardships. I'd been warned that I'd lose my teeth, so I made self-care imperative from that point on. (Many predicaments have had to be addressed; I still have my teeth, though!) I carried with me the message that seemed to be continually passed along stemming from my attempting suicide: that it was my own fault, I was to blame, and worst of all...that I was a bad person.

There was a certain stigma placed upon people who'd been in mental hospitals. The halfway house permitted residents to bring in audio equipment, so I could finally listen to my music again! A line from one song literally saved me from the stigmatization: *"Never trust the eyes of one who causes you shame."* I breathed these words as my oxygen. Most of the folks at the halfway house had been there for many years, as if it were a "whole-way" house. I was hoping to one day move on.

Because of the years spent in hospitals, I had no college degrees or skills. I felt inferior to my peers. One important lesson that I then taught myself and that I'd like to share with you is this: compare yourself only to yourself. When I compared myself to other people in their 20s, I felt like I couldn't measure up or ever catch up. When I changed this to comparing myself to how I'd been, I felt some pride. I was doing things I was told I probably would never be able to do. Plus, I was no longer in a mental institution!

My intelligence was still with me, even though I had no letters after my name. I decided to try getting a volunteer job at the hospital that "reconstructed" me. I was accepted! Not long thereafter, I was told that a paid position had opened up with me in mind. They wanted me to be the unit coordinator for the Division of Behavioral Medicine.

Wow! Let's stop here for a minute. Debby, the director of volunteers, knew that the address I'd entered on my application form was a halfway house, yet she believed in me and took a chance on me. This changed the course of my life, just as seeking help as an adolescent had changed it in the opposite way. All of us can try to be like Debby. We may not hold positions of power, but we can try in our own ways to be accepting and inclusive.

It felt weird to hold the unit coordinator position while living in a halfway house. Soon, I got a little apartment and moved out on my own. The choice was between two apartments—one much closer to the hospital than the other. I chose the one farther away. Eventually, I decided I didn't want to be in and around hospitals if I didn't have to be, so I sought another job. This time, I had a resumé to present and an address that wasn't a halfway house. I found a job as the administrative assistant at a health-related charitable foundation around the corner from my apartment.

PART TWO

5

"Sun Is Shining"

(Extended Club Mix)

by

Bob Marley

+ Funkstar De Luxe

I was 26. Ten years had passed since my first suicide attempt. I yearned for companionship. Here again, I felt concerned about not being "enough." I was still unhealed from all that led to my suicide attempts and from what followed. I also had substantial issues regarding my body image. With most of my tongue burned away and the remainder immobile, lips made from skin grafts, a mouth with very restrictive opening, scars from the skin grafts and the gastrostomy incision and a closed hole where the tube had been, I felt considerable self-consciousness. Because of previous experiences, I'd taught myself since youth not to see people's body but to see their essence instead and to disassociate myself from my body. From childhood, I'd known that I didn't want to give birth/have kids. I was (and am) no gender. I also was (and am) no sexual label. This felt different from the world around me. All I wanted (and still want) was humanness—love in the form of deep, emotional connection as a human with a human.

Each day, when I walked home from work to my apartment, I'd see a guy jogging with Walkman headphones ensconced and wobbling amidst his thick, gray curls as he sang reggae while he ran. It was a sight to behold, yet I seemed to be the only one noticing. He was different from the rest of the people who were rushing without acknowledging other pedestrians. As we passed one another, we'd smile and wave. This went on for a while (I forget how many days/weeks) until one day he stopped, introduced himself, asked me my name and if he could walk with me.

We walked until we got to my apartment. He said he felt a connection with me because I seemed friendly. He'd not encountered any other approachable people. Here was another instance where being inclusive made a difference. He asked if I'd like to walk around the reservoir with him that weekend. I thought, *"Oh no, he'd probably want to learn more about me. Should I say okay?"* I wanted so badly to try to accept myself and be open to possibilities, so I said, "*Yes.*"

We met at the reservoir and began our stroll. He shared his life history with me. I have to tell you, it was serendipitous how our lives had similar occurrences at the same time.

Leon grew up in Chicago. He'd had a rough upbringing in which he'd been beaten repetitively by a housekeeper. She used weighty wooden hangers, saying she'd beat Leon and his younger brother until they cried. The little brother cried the second he saw a hanger. In order to protect his brother, Leon took the beatings (usually to his torso but sometimes to his head) and would never cry. He found solace with friends, playing together. He put himself through school, married, had children, and was trying to build a career as a CPA. He explained that in those days (the 1950s), people were expected to start families in their twenties, and his marriage had been based on practicality. At age 30, he found a position that required moving to Massachusetts, which he did right around the time I was born.

Leon worked hard for that company for years until it closed down. He found another job as an internal auditor for a company that owned several subsidiaries. While he was on the mezzanine overseeing the production of aluminum pots and pans, he had a seizure, fell off the mezzanine, and just missed landing in a huge vat of boiling aluminum. This happened at the same time I had my life-altering suicide attempt.

Leon was diagnosed with epilepsy, which came from scarring on his brain from the beatings. He was told he could no longer work and had to apply for disability. His identity was being stripped away from him. In those days, surgery was done to try to stop seizure activity. His skull was drilled into, and part of the temporal lobe of his brain was removed. After surgery, he was told: he had lost fields of vision, his medications would cause extreme drowsiness and erectile dysfunction, he'd have a form of dysphasia that would cause him to think he was saying one thing but to actually say the opposite word, and his emotions would be different (but they didn't offer any further explanation). He had his brain surgery while I was having my reconstructive surgery and skin grafts.

Leon's marriage, which had been troubled for years, had begun unraveling when he couldn't work. Then it fell apart. He and his wife divorced and sold their house. He moved to the town I'd chosen for the halfway house at the same time I moved there. Had I not chosen the apartment I picked, we'd have never crossed each other's paths.

Every event in our lives and every choice we made brought us to the spot where we met. Leon found me. As I shared my history with him, he didn't judge me. None of my limitations discouraged him. Leon and I were both misfits, but we fit together. This was a miracle. Each of us had been derailed, but our paths merged—and we both allowed ourselves to accept and welcome human connection. When I walked home, I could feel the sunshine for the first time in my life.

We started to spend time together, walking (usually holding hands and skipping) to parks and playing all sorts of games. Playing with his pals had been what pulled Leon through his early life. I had such a compelling longing to play, but had often been excluded. This was my chance, so I'd pack a knapsack with different games for us. I had tennis and badminton gear, nerf and beach balls, an assortment of card games, Backgammon, Hangman, Trivial Pursuit, Parcheesi, Monopoly, Clue, and the collection was growing! We even made up some of our own guessing games. When we played, we didn't compete. With badminton, for example, we'd try to hit the birdie back and forth for as many times as we could to keep it from falling. Our record was 123! When we played Trivial Pursuit, we'd teach each other and learn together. When it came time for getting each other gifts, new games were the choice. The best one we ever found was called The Quest of the Philosopher's Stone. If a game required being opponents, our love of play was the winner.

For me, play was/is therapeutic. Let me explain. Being playful is associated with freedom and spontaneity; it doesn't have a set structure. It is creative. The interactions therein can be unpredictable and profound. It is guided by the moment. Playing games allows people to experience some of the benefits of being playful with the safety of structure and predictability. This is medicinal for those of us with anxiety, obsessiveness, and attention issues. The games represent a world we can enter that is safe, within our control, challenging, and fun. We can master the game and feel sure of our moves. We can try new strategies without risking anything critical. We can feel at peace while we play, as if the world of the game is THE world. No problems exist. They are elsewhere. We are in the moment, thinking only of the game and protected by it. This can be the only time some of us can feel any semblance of peace. The moves can be both creative and transformative. The mind is actively engaged so that the body can be relieved of tension. This is so healthy! Because of the comfort zone the game provides, a connection between players can reach unexplored depths. This is what unfolded for me with Leon. I could see into his soul while playing with him because I was feeling unencumbered and safe.

The next thing I gave him was my favorite book—<u>The Little Prince</u>. He didn't just read it. He studied it, and he wrote pages of notes about it. That was when I knew he was my soulmate.

We decided to find a place to live together. He taught me about mortgages and familiarized me with lots of practical life skills. Don't forget, I'd been in a completely different world for a decade. He showed me light—which direction the sun rose and set, and how important light can be in the home. I'd been in darkness for so many years, this was enlightening! Like the little prince, we'd watch the sunset every evening. We dressed alike in jeans and sweatshirts, often matching. Music was always with us, and we'd dance if the spirit moved us. He wrote poems for me. Our togetherness was the first experience of deep love for each of us.

Eventually, we discussed marriage. Neither of us felt a legal document mattered, but I thought it might be important to get married because I was 30 years younger than he and wanted him to know I'd stay as he got old. We wrote a poem together for our wedding. Here it is:

nightfall
the sun is nowhere to be seen
darkness lays heavily upon the souls
there is no path to daylight

early dawn
the sunlight is scant
mist lingers dankly amid entwined branches
the path is difficult to find

mid-morning
the sun rises gracefully
dew sparkles upon the fresh ground
the path is clearing

high noon
the sun is beaming
warmth fills all hearts
the path has been found

dusk
the sun sets gently
lustrous colors stream across the sky
the path glows with peace, gratitude, and love

He'd make my breakfast each morning and include a note inside my napkin. He'd take care of the household chores, grocery shopping, and cooking, etc. while I went to work. He performed these routine tasks with extraordinary joy. For example, when he'd fold the laundry, he'd have our sweatshirts be arm in arm. When I came home from work, we'd have supper, watch MacNeil-Lehrer,

Jeopardy, then play or watch another show or movie, and cuddle. When we'd watch a show or movie, we'd be intertwined. If the content was sad, I'd cry—but he couldn't. He'd never cried since those beatings. He'd gently wipe a tear from my cheek and place it on his.

He understood about my difficulty eating and tried to come up with meals that would work. When I got alarming infections in my mouth from using forks to move the food so it could be chewed, I had to endure surgery in which laser was used to burn away the lesions (more burning). Leon then had a fabulous idea: instead of using metal forks, use plastic ones. He'd buy them and use an emery board to file the sides if any were sharp.

When we went shopping together, we'd find ourselves dancing in the aisles to whatever Muzak was coming through the sound system. Although neither of us had healed from our past experiences, we were truly happy together in the present moment!

6

"Heart of the Sunrise"

by

Yes

My job at the health-related charitable foundation had been going well, except they had decided to move. It felt too far for me to commute daily. Leon had met the director and had a proposal for him. The director clicked with Leon because someone close to him also had epilepsy. He liked Leon's knowledge of accounting. Leon suggested that I do the bookkeeping as an independent contractor, and the director initiated our new venture. Leon taught me how to do the accounting for charitable foundations. He gave me a profession.

We found a little office near our condo, and we named the new business A.S. Accounting Services. Before you knew it, lots of health-related charitable organizations requested to be clients as did other businesses and individuals. Leon taught me everything I needed to know. The work itself was quite beneficial for me. It was soothing to have columns for everything and to have one correct answer that I could get right without obsessing or having to do any lengthy reading. I called what was occurring "creative compensation." In spite of the encephalitis, years in hospitals instead of college, and loss of most of my tongue, with Leon's help I found a way to be participating in the world. This became a valued part of my identity.

Leon had been advised that the stress of working could cause seizures for him, so I did the work in the office while he was at home available to call if I needed his expertise. Neither of us had an understanding about Leon's brain surgery nor about the impact stress could have on him and how it would reveal itself. I also did not have a full grasp of all that had happened with me.

Accounting questions came up that I needed to ask Leon. Because of his dysphasia, the words that came out as answers were often the opposite of what he thought he was saying. How would I know? Sometimes I'd ask again because it felt confusing. Other times, I didn't know enough to even be confused. I felt concerned for the clients and worried for myself. When I shared this with Leon, he seemed ashamed at first but this quickly shifted to angry harshness. I was taken completely off guard. When I tried to discuss his reaction, he said that I'd provoked him. My greatest vulnerability is invalidation, and here it was. Somehow we'd both been struck in our Achilles heels. We couldn't comprehend this. We were each stuck in our own woundedness without understanding how to help ourselves or each other. I think we were both seeking protection for ourselves.

We tried our damnedest to hold onto our love and togetherness with all the activities we shared, but there was an elephant in the room. The stress began to mount as A.S. Accounting Services continued to grow and demanded more of my time. Then Leon's verbal lashing out could include throwing objects or putting a fist through a wall. If only I knew then what I know now. I can't stand writing this about my dear soulmate. Let me cheat and tell you what I do know now. I'll then tell the rest of the story.

What I recently learned is that Leon had traumatic brain injury. Stress caused him to react in ways he couldn't control. It wasn't just the business that caused the problem. It seemed to come from any stressful situation. I wish he had received some helpful information about the complications of his brain surgery so that he wouldn't have felt ashamed and defensive. I wish I'd known so we could've been a team dealing with this together instead of my taking it personally and feeling defenseless.

Years passed, and we continued playing, dancing, holding hands while skipping, and cuddling while watching shows. There was always a note in my napkin at breakfast. We still loved each other with all our hearts. When stress arose, so did the scary behavior. The behavior was taking its toll on each of our inner sprits, but we didn't have a way to address this. We were never able to connect the dots; we didn't know that the behavior was out of Leon's control.

7

"World In Changes"

(from Certified Live)

by

Dave Mason

Ten years into our marriage, Leon wanted to move to a smaller town with a slower pace. There were some problems with our condo and the town was feeling more like a city. I understood and agreed to move, but I was hesitant about leaving the place where we'd met and built a life. I was also concerned about giving up the structure of having an office. In addition, what we loved about the town where we were living was its walkability. We lived walking distance from the office, shops, restaurants, parks, and the library.

When we put our condo on the market, we must've priced it too low because it sold right away. We didn't have a place to go. We discovered that most towns that weren't rural had highways and malls. The only place I knew where one could walk to lots of spots was where I grew up. We'd been going there a few times a year for holiday functions, but I tried to steer clear otherwise. Whenever we went, I was confronted with memories that I didn't have the wherewithal to handle. This time, we went without a formal invitation; we just took ourselves on an excursion. That day, I saw my hometown area through Leon's eyes. He seemed enamored with it. He still jogged everyday (like when I first met him), and relished doing so along the seashore. We found a rental apartment that very day. When we packed up, our "heavy stuff" (both the furniture and the relationship issues) came with us.

Moving back was daunting. Being in close proximity to where the problems of my youth snowballed into an avalanche was chilling and caused me to face the problems head on. I hadn't been out and about the area since I was an adolescent. Here I was known, but hadn't been seen since my suicide attempts. I routinely felt like I was being viewed as a disgrace. I had a lot of reconciliation work ahead of me.

I never thought I'd be able to come back, but with Leon by my side I could...and we deepened our relationship with even more shared activities. We got an inflatable dinghy and rowed back and forth in the harbor. To us, it was like being on a yacht! There was an expansive park nearby where we played badminton without a net. That's where we reached 123 hits without the birdie falling. We'd give each other a sweaty hug after each long volley. When indoors, we played "mini-pong." This is ping-pong with a miniature table and special paddles. We'd play with reggae accompanying us in the background. Leon had cute nicknames for things: mini-pong was Minnie, the microwave oven was Mickey, the VCR was Vicki. He had a top hat and every so often he'd don it and appear from around a wall tipping his hat to greet me

Leon and I developed a burgeoning appreciation for the area. We delighted in attending live performances at the Little Theater, dancing at outdoor performing arts concerts, and partaking in various festivals. We felt a sense of belonging. However, sometimes when people recognized me they'd point me out, and I could hear them commenting to one another about what I'd done.

Feeling like a "bad person" was something I'd not yet overcome. How I ached to do so. Being back "at the scene" was an opportunity to honestly examine that feeling and to locate the inner strength to confront it. My determination led me to the synagogue I attended as a youngster. Somehow I felt that this could be the place where I could feel like a "good person" if I did good deeds. This could also help to recreate the structure that was missing from giving up the A.S. Accounting Services office for a home office with weekly pick-ups and drop-offs to clients without live contact. Volunteering at the Temple could help me be with people. If I did mitzvot (good deeds), maybe people would accept me and my history.

The executive director, Judith, remembered me from years ago. She seemed to fully surmise what I was seeking even though I didn't actually verbalize it. Judith was like Debby, but even more commendable because she knew my history. She genuinely wanted to give me a chance, and at the same time envisioned how the Temple could benefit from my contributions.

Judith had a knack for matching people's talents with tasks that needed fulfillment. One of the offshoots of my having had encephalitis was/is an enhanced recognition and memory of details (as opposed to lengthy written material). Any work that's concrete involving details feels comforting to me. Judith offered me the meaningful project of acknowledging donations and sending death anniversary notices. Doing these connected me to the recipients as I became aware of their celebrations and their losses. Another outgrowth of my having had encephalitis was/is neatly-detailed handwriting, which led me to learn calligraphy. Judith appointed me as the scribe for Temple certificates. Inscribing these connected me to the kids and their families. The Temple Library became my "spot" in which to work three days a week on the many volunteer tasks presented to me. When I'd come home, I'd see a curly gray head bobbing up and down. It was Leon, excited to see me! He and I attended Sabbath services together every Friday evening. We both joined the chorus, too.

I was doing what I could to help myself feel like a "good person" instead of a bad one. In addition to volunteering at the Temple, I took a weekly volunteer shift at the Counseling Center answering phones and doing office work. I also volunteered at the Public Library delivering books to homebound elders. In the town where Leon and I met, it had been just the two of us in anonymity. My only activity there had been A.S. Accounting Services. Here, we were part of the community. I'm not sure Leon felt comfortable with this. He was more of a loner. I think he may have had a hard time getting used to my being involved with organizations and other people. Looking back on it, I can see that for Leon this was a monumental change. How I wish I perceived this then. I was so enmeshed in trying to become a "good person" that I couldn't discern how it was affecting the person closest to me.

In the meantime, we found a condo in the center of town—walking distance to everything—and made a permanent home for ourselves. It had a deck which became our all-time favorite place to play games. The park was right at the bottom of our hill. We'd eagerly skip there hand in hand for hours of fun. I continued to diligently do my clients' work and my volunteer work. Leon continued to lovingly maintain the household. There was always a note in my napkin every morning and cuddling in the evening while watching shows. We were attached like Velcro.

I wasn't cognizant of the added layer of stress I'd put on the marriage with my need to be a "good person," plus the stress that came from moving and renovating. None of this was good for Leon's situation, and his symptoms became more frequent (but, don't forget, we didn't know the cause of the behavior). During this time, I increased my responsibilities at the Temple by becoming the librarian. I also became a member of the town's AIDS Awareness Committee.

Then the tragedy of Columbine took place. I wrote a letter to the editor of our local newspaper:

Is Compassion Possible?

The Columbine tragedy hit me in a way that compels me to write this letter, with hopes that maybe, just maybe, I can be of some form of help.

You see, I was a young person in emotional turmoil. As an adolescent, I resorted to violence, against myself only, thankfully. The pain inside took over. It literally took control of my being and my actions. A numbness usurped my body, allowing me to endure any act of horror inflicted upon me. Is it possible that the two students in Columbine felt this same type of pain?

In my case, I believe I tried reaching out, even crying out for help before trying to take my life. Somehow, my pleas weren't understood. Is it possible that the two students in Columbine sent the same distress signals that weren't understood?

We may not be able to know the degree of another person's pain, nor what the appropriate intervention might be, if any. I strongly believe, however, that all of us—regardless of our age or gender, sexual orientation, religion, race, income, profession, education, or political views—can choose to live compassionately. We can try to stop putting people down. We can try to stop labeling and making assumptions about people. We can try to stop judging. We can try to be in touch with our own pain, so that when we see another person in pain, we can offer love and concern. Is it possible?

A teen task force was formed in town, and I was asked to be on it because of the letter I'd written. My involvement felt like a turning point for me. I was on the side of extending help instead of requesting it. The meetings discussing safety in our schools caused me to remember how unsafe I had felt at my school.

Then I had an idea that I thought was a breakthrough, but it ended up breaking my life apart. How I wish I'd known then about the magnitude of its consequences. The idea was to make an appointment at the school to seek validation and understanding about what had happened decades ago with the teacher. I thought it would be possible to do so without hurting anyone.

During the meeting, I was treated with kindness and given everything I'd hoped to find. Afterwards, when higher authorities were notified, all of this was withdrawn and replaced by harshness and the need for legal assistance, as I was warned that I could be sued for defamation of character. My hope for healing that had taken decades to find had disappeared. I was counseled to put a homestead exemption on the deed to our condo and was advised to discontinue any action regarding the matter with the teacher. I never wanted to pursue anything more than healing. All I sought was compassion. I didn't comprehend the way the system worked. Had I known, I never would have gone back to the school.

8

"In Two Minds"

by

Riverside

I was distraught over the school situation. The tension from my integrity being threatened had been demoralizing, and the agitation from worrying about being sued had been debilitating. The absolute worst aspect was its effect on Leon. The stress was the most we had ever had, and I was the most vulnerable I'd been since we met. This time, when his scary behavior came, I asked if we could go for help. He contemplated this notion and wrote pages of notes about it. He shared his notes with me and explained that he thought he'd rather leave. I was stunned. I honestly didn't know what hit me.

The notes listed what he loved about our present life together. There were no negatives except my inability to travel and his wanting to go less frequently to synagogue. Then he wrote that: his past is a logjam, and the future requires him to make major changes. He delineated: "*When the major changes are considered, it is so much easier to 'get out from under'—to live as I am, bothering no one—to permit the past to remain in the past and to move on—selfish but true."* I didn't grasp then that asking him to address the present behavior would probably require him to reopen his past, the thought of which was putting him in harm's way.

Neither of us could absorb what was transpiring. We each were in our own emotional fallout shelter, rendering both of us unable to think clearly. I begged Leon to stay. I told him he didn't have to get help. This caused me ambivalence. He must've felt something similar because he said he felt that the problem was like a guillotine over his head, and as much as he loved our life together, he had to go. I begged him so much to stay that he called himself Shane (like in the Western when the little boy yells, *"Shane, come back,"* as the cowboy rides off into the sunset).

On Memorial Day, our town held its annual Great Picnic. It was the first activity we had attended together when we moved here, and it was our last. I know that day I made him aware of how much I loved him and how I couldn't bear his leaving. I literally fell to the ground as we neared the entrance. My legs gave way. I wept next to him. He put his arm around me and took care of me.

One of his kids had been transferred out of state, so he thought that was where he should move. I drove him to and from the airport when he went to check it out. I helped him fill out his apartment application. We were still doing all the things we loved together. There was still a note in my napkin every morning. He was really leaving, but it wasn't registering for either of us. Since he was going far away, we thought it made sense to get a divorce. The piece of paper never mattered to us. Thinking back, I remember getting married so he'd feel secure as he aged. Now I was the one being left.

Nothing was sinking in. Even our going to court for the divorce was like an outing for us. We held hands on the way in and on the way out. Boxes were being packed. I'd see them in the corners of our rooms and my heart would skip a beat, but I couldn't believe that what they represented was real. He didn't pack anything except his clothes. He wanted me to have everything else. We took photos of him doing his favorite activities here. I made an album of the photographs for each of us.

For our last days together, I asked that we go to all our special spots to say goodbye to them with one another. We went back to the town where we met, to the reservoir, to the park, to the office, and to our former apartments and condos. We did the same thing in the town to which we moved and included doing our cherished activities: we skipped while holding hands to the apartment we'd rented, we played badminton without a net in the park, we paddled in our inflatable "yacht" at the harbor, and we watched the sun set over the ocean. As the orange ball was dropping beyond the horizon, I looked into Leon's eyes beseechingly and felt his soul. I had a glimpse for a millisecond into the future. At the time, I discounted it completely and thought I was a kook. The glimmer saw Leon dying. When we got home, we played Trivial Pursuit out on the deck while there was still some light. Then we played mini-pong inside with reggae to dance to between rounds. After that, we read <u>The Little Prince</u>. I was choked up while I read it to him. As midnight approached, we played our favorite game: The Quest of the Philosopher's Stone. I reached out to Leon before he went to sleep, and he said he felt like one of us was dying.

The next morning (June 29th), my final napkin note was displayed. It read: "*I love you and I always will.*" I drove Leon to the airport. In the car, I gave each of us the photo album. With his, I included a little polished stone and a copy of our wedding poem. We then read what we'd written for our wedding just as we did back then, alternating verses and reading the last one in unison: *The path glows with peace, gratitude, and love.* I was crying. I knew he couldn't cry. We hugged and said we love each other. He got out and headed to the terminal. I waited until he was in the door and then drove. I was numb. When I got home, there was a message from Leon on the answering machine:

"*I did cry as I saw the gray car pull away. I love you. I thank you so much for today, for the last few days, for the last few weeks, and for the entire time I've known you. I'll talk to you again. I love you. Bye.*"

He cried. After over 60 years, he finally could cry. As sad as I was, that brought me something I couldn't define back then.

9

"Tears"

by

Rush

I was broken. It felt like I'd plummeted into a chasm. I couldn't detect any light. It dawned on me that during the span of our 14-year marriage I had never been alone except for a few weekends when Leon visited his family out of state. He'd been with me for my whole adult life since the hospitals and halfway house. In the blink of an eye, I was living a solitary existence. I was surrounded by everything Leon and I had shared. I'd come home expecting the bouncing curly gray hair to greet me, then get stung by the reality of his departure. I'd walk up and down our hill without being able to skip while holding hands. I'd look out onto the deck to see where we'd played, and I ached that this therapeutic aspect of life was no longer readily available to me. The park seemed like a vacant expanse without him. Mini-pong and all of our other games were gathering dust.

I did try to find an activity that could be done alone, and I got a bike. Cycling became an integral part of my life. One day while riding, I saw a double rainbow. I immediately rode home to show Leon. I entered the empty dwelling and collapsed in despair when I remembered he'd gone.

People who used to see us holding hands skipping around town would stop and ask me where Leon was. I couldn't form the words to adequately answer. My response was awkward because I'd never been able to assimilate Leon's changes in behavior; they were the exact opposite of the way he usually was. When Leon left, I sometimes seemed to block out those episodes. Other times I'd remind myself that I had to reach out for us to seek help. When I saw his consternation I let go of that plan, but I was still mired in regret and felt that I'd failed. I was blaming myself and not supporting my need for healing.

The majority of the world around me seemed to treat me as though nothing had changed in my life. This was one of the most distressing aspects and tapped into my unhealed self. I wanted to die. What kept me alive was not wanting to be viewed as a "bad person" for committing suicide and not wanting to hurt anybody.

I called Leon a lot. Oh, I missed him more than words could describe. He called me also. We agreed that we still loved each other and were each other's special person even though we were no longer living together. He said he was disoriented. He shared that he'd been calling other people my nicknames by mistake. He'd been remembering our being intertwined while watching TV, but he said he was trying not to focus on the past.

I'd often ask why he left because I was continually wondering if there was something I could have done differently that would have stopped him. He'd reply that: he caused difficulties, he couldn't give what he once did, he got into a mode of behavior that he couldn't break, he had a certain mindset and nothing I could have done would have made a difference. Even though he said these things, I kept feeling it was my fault he left. I perseverated on the apprehension that I had made some huge mistakes: that I never should have gone back to the school—that I shouldn't have focused on Leon's behavior, which would've required him to confront his past—that I should have been less critical of him—that I shouldn't have let him go—that I should have tried harder to keep him here.

The divorce papers came in the mail stating it was finalized. We each put our copies of the documents in a drawer. Summer had become autumn. It was time to bring the deck furniture down to the basement. There used to be a shadow of both of us on the deck, now there was only mine. Every sunset reminded me of Leon. He had brought the furniture up. I was carrying it down. Leon would never again bring it back up. I was so sad that I seemed to proceed in slow-motion. The most fun and peace I ever had was out on the deck with him.

On Halloween, I remembered playing cards with him as we waited for trick-or-treaters last year. This year, I was sitting by myself on the raw, dreary night. I felt such an ache inside. I called and asked Leon to please come home. He changed the subject.

Soon it would be Leon's 70th birthday. I had turned 40 a few months before he left. We always used to change his age on my birthday so we'd have the second number matching. I sent him a card, a selection of his favorite music, and a copy of The Little Prince. Here's what the card said:

"If I could reach up and hold a star for every time you've made me smile, the entire evening sky would be in the palm of my hand. Happy Birthday to my treasured friend. You're finally really 70. Now you won't have to advance your age on March 17th anymore. I send you my love and sincerest wishes for your happiness."

He called in the morning on his birthday while I was still asleep and left me a message:

"*I opened it up. Oh my God, what a beautiful, beautiful gift. The card was magnificent. The songs and The Little Prince. My eyes watered when I saw it. All the time I was feeling the package, I thought it was a picture of some sort, and I thought, oh wow, where am I gonna put it, you know? And then when I opened the package and saw the title, my eyes just filled with water. It was just marvelous. It's gonna stay right near me. I love it. Thank you so much. And the songs. I'm gonna listen and listen and listen. Beautiful. I'll never forget 'em. Thank you. Love you. Bye.*"

I was deeply touched by the way he described tears and how they seemed to be connected with our love. When I called him back, he said he was an ogre for leaving. He expressed a desire to come visit and see me again. I didn't think I could handle seeing him and then having him leave again.

10

"In the Middle of the Night"

by

Joseph Arthur

Shortly after his birthday, Leon told me about his finding new doctors. When he was here with me, his doctors declared that he was a specimen of health for his age. He jogged eight miles a day and ate a balanced diet. While we were together, he never got sick except for an occasional cold and the flu we both caught before learning about the vaccine. Other than routine EEGs, the only time he was in the hospital was when his finger got mangled in the pull-out sofa bed and required surgery to reattach it.

Aside from the epilepsy, Leon had a common heart murmur called mitral valve prolapse. It wasn't serious and just required taking antibiotics before dental appointments. Even though he wasn't experiencing any symptoms, the new doctor informed him that he should have it operated on. The physician said that his heart was enlarging; if he didn't have the operation, he soon wouldn't be able to jog—and if he did have it, he'd be guaranteed many years of vigor.

I asked Leon if he wanted to call our close friend who was a cardiologist to get another opinion. He said he was too embarrassed to call because he'd left me. He felt he'd lucked out with his new doctors. I told people that leaving me and moving away was saving his life. He scheduled the surgery in the first available open slot (which would be in January) because he didn't want anything looming over him.

Winter was approaching with its darkness and cold temperatures. When it snowed here, Leon said he felt protective of me. He found an advertisement for the matching slippers (he called them slippies) we'd been wearing for all these years and ordered new ones for each of us. He said he was reevaluating his life. When I asked again about being with me, he didn't shrug it off.

He had to have some tests that would be taken through his esophagus. I could empathize completely and felt achingly sorrowful for him. He was having trouble keeping track of all the appointments. I used to do that for him. I asked if he wanted me there. At that point, he said he needed me to stop discussing the relationship. He couldn't think of anything except his physical situation, and my being there would be too complicated.

The holidays came and went—my first alone in many years. Emptiness was what was present for me. As a way to fill it up a bit, I bought blankets and wrapped them with sweets attached to the ribbon, and then delivered the packages to the homeless. Their gratitude was a true gift, but my desolation was impenetrable.

My slippers arrived on the day Leon entered the hospital. The operation would be the next morning. I was the person he wanted to speak with on the night before his surgery. He said he was wondering if we'll ever see each other again. When I thanked him for the slippers, he was concerned that his pair wouldn't be delivered because he wasn't home. That's what worried him! We gave each other our love, and I gave him my best wishes for his surgery. My heart was melting when I thought of him in the hospital and when I looked at those cute slippers.

The next day, I couldn't stop thinking about him as he was being operated on. It made sense to feel close to a loved one when he underwent surgery. It hurt me beyond words to feel cut off from him while he was experiencing life and death issues.

That night, he was awake in cardiac intensive care after the surgery that repaired the valve. He'd be there for several days, then moved to a hospital room for a few more days. The breathing tube was out. He had a sore throat, but otherwise wasn't in a lot of pain. I felt like he should be coming home now; he'd been gone long enough. When we spoke he actually said, "*When I see you...*"

Later, he described the surgery: He was sawed down the middle from the bottom of his neck to his belly button. Wires woven between the halves of his sternum would stay in forever for the bone to grow back together. Skin was sewn below the surface with dissolving stitches. During surgery, they picked up an irregularity in his heartbeat which had to be monitored. Clotting medication would be necessary for one month. There'd be no driving for one month, and he couldn't go outdoors unless the temperature was above 40 degrees. He was now ambulatory and disconnected from machines.

When he was back at his apartment, I called several times a day. He was often looking out his window while we talked, wishing he could soon resume jogging. One day I was vacuuming and moved a hamper that I usually leave in place. There I found a bunch of Leon's gray curls. I got choked up and called to tell him about finding them. I took that opportunity to thank him for the thoughtful way he used to clean and take care of our home. When not wearing the new slippers, I kept them next to my desk until he got discharged. His slippers had arrived safely, and we were both wearing our new pairs now.

He'd been home from the hospital for about two weeks when I noticed a persistent little cough during our phone conversation. I suggested that he call the doctor. He said that he had called and left a message. Then he said he'd been feeling lightheaded also. He called the doctor's office several times over the next two days about this as well, but hadn't heard back. He tried again the following day (Valentine's Day) to no avail. This was really bothering me. If I'd been there, I'd have taken him to the doctor. On the fourth day, when I checked in to see if the doctor finally called him, he was in a panic. He insisted that I get off the line because he needed the doctor to get through. He said he thought he was going to have a stroke. A while later, he called and told me he was glad I was there. He said the doctor's office finally called him back. They thought it was probably the Coumadin (blood thinner) level needing to be increased and made an appointment for noon the next day.

When I called that night, his voice was frail. I asked if he had anything to eat. He said he couldn't make it to the kitchen, but had some oatmeal squares near where he was sitting. He marveled at how fast the characters on the television were moving. His speech seemed so slow. I wanted to call 911, but he said they told him he was supposed to feel this weak. He said he was relieved that he had the appointment the next day. I then asked if we could please be together. He said, "*Sure*."

11

"Gone Away"

by

Ziggy Marley

& the Melody Makers

I didn't know that his loving answer to my heartfelt question would be the last word he ever uttered. He died at 10:00 AM—so he never made it to the noon appointment. I was devastated. I still couldn't believe that Leon left, and now he had died. I couldn't bear being separated from him and not being by his side when he had open heart surgery (and all he had to undergo by himself without help from his doctor)—and now he was dead. The doctor was also shocked and sorry too, but he hadn't received information from the office staff so didn't know that Leon should have been seen sooner. If I'd been with him, I would have surely taken him to be checked.

I'd been telling everyone that leaving saved his life. Now the reverse seemed true—it took his life away. My going back to the school to seek compassion had seemed so positive at first. I thought something of mine finally counted. But revisiting what had occurred there nearly killed me, and it did kill my marriage; now I blamed it for killing

Leon. I felt Leon's death was my fault. My yearning for healing caused him to feel he had to leave, and then he died.

He'd been gone for only seven months. The first two didn't feel real. It was as though he'd gone on a vacation. Then autumn came, and I couldn't stop crying and asking him to come home. I continually inquired about why he left, and if it was because of me. With news of his heart issues in late autumn, I stopped discussing anything concerning myself. Then winter came and the surgery, recuperation, and death.

Our love had been restored to its original innocence when Leon had surgery. He even wanted us to be together again. When he died, the love deepened beyond earthly description. I would've given anything for him to have life again, even if without me. I ascertained right then and there that the deep-seated fear from my teenage years would prevent me from taking my own life, but living without Leon on this planet felt inconceivable.

For me, Leon's leaving and dying were like a double death. The leaving made the death worse. However, to most of the people around me, his leaving delegitimized his dying. The reaction of many had been, "*He was already gone.*" This crippled me. It felt as though I was reliving the injurious invalidation from my early years. No funeral was held for him, since hardly anyone where he'd moved knew him. I had no rights because of the divorce, so I couldn't make a funeral for him. There was no closure for me, no ritual to bring sympathy to me, and no memorial for him. I did write an obituary for the local newspaper. Figuring out how to word it was grueling, but these two lines from it brought me solace:

Leon loved jogging as the sun rose each morning and gazing at the sky as the sun set each evening. He felt music in his soul, from Mozart to Marley.

The town was seeking donors for park benches, so I bought one at the park where we played badminton without a net. This was the closest thing I could find to resemble a gravesite or cemetery. Here's what I came up with for the plaque:

IN LOVING MEMORY OF

LEON WISEL

AND OUR JOY TOGETHER

People who hadn't seen me for a while would ask where Leon was when they saw me walking without him holding my hand and skipping along. Now I had to disclose that he died. The people who'd been told he'd left didn't know he'd died unless they read the obituary or I had the chance to explain. It was disheartening and disorienting. I couldn't keep track of who knew what.

I missed him so much when he left. Now I couldn't begin to quantify the degree to which I missed him, and I couldn't call him anymore. I realized that when we had talked, we'd actually been mourning together the loss of our marriage. Now I was grief-stricken and thrown into confinement with it.

PART THREE

12

"Unbound"

by

Robbie Robertson

A month after Leon died came my birthday. Before he died, I'd been eagerly wondering what he'd send to me. He wasn't able to go out. This was before online shopping, so I knew there wouldn't be a gift. To my surprise, a big box arrived at my doorstep. It wasn't from Leon, but it contained his possessions. It had the clothes I'd watched him pack. They were back, but without him. There was the photo album, our wedding poem, the stone, the order form for the new slippers (he died wearing his), the birthday card I'd sent him, the songs, and The Little Prince with a watermark where his tear had fallen. I wept uncontrollably.

I played and replayed the songs. I made CDs with them and his voice messages that I'd saved. I'd writhe woefully on the floor as I listened, then start again.

I dug out the philosophical notes he'd written about The Little Prince all those years ago. I was struck by the prophetic and illuminating nature of this section of his notes:

"*The apparent sad departure of the little prince in no way alters love. It is a reiteration of the oneness of love; the ultimate maturation of two into one. The common spirit is represented by one remaining being.*"

I didn't know then that these words would be my inspirational guide one day. At this juncture, I was overrun by grief. I did have an experience shortly after digging up his notes that I'd like to impart to you. If I hadn't been inundated with regret and self-blame, it would've brought me consolation at that time. It did years later, though. Here it is:

Leon's favorite musical genre was calypso and his favorite Sabbath song was Shalom Rav (abundant peace). Right after reading those Little Prince notes, I went to services at the synagogue. The musician who wrote Shalom Rav was a guest that evening. He said he had a special surprise for us—he was going to play

Shalom Rav with a calypso beat. I started crying and couldn't stop throughout the service because Leon was missing this.

The next day, I took a bike ride. On the path near the Temple, something was being conveyed to me. It wasn't with words, but it felt like a communication of some sort. What I deciphered was: "Amy, why'd you have to cry through the whole Shalom Rav in calypso?—I couldn't hear it!"

That stopped me in my tracks. I was the remaining being on this plane of existence, living for both of us.

On June 29th, one year after Leon had moved away, I drove to the airport. I parked in the lot and walked into the terminal where his flight had been. I went to the pay phone (we didn't have cell phones yet) where he'd left me the message saying he cried. I went back to the car and sobbed. When I got home, I pulled out the fan to cool off the condo. The cord was still wrapped neatly, the way Leon had left it. I found one of his gray curls in the twist tie. This was so different from when I had found his curls behind the hamper and called him. Now it felt like I'd found a treasured relic.

I was stuck in a loop. I'd diligently do my clients' work or my volunteer work, then return home to the emptiness. There was no one with me to share memories of Leon. I had emulated the way Leon took care of the household chores, but couldn't seem to adjust to living without him. I'd miss him, and then immediately feel it was my fault that he left and died. I couldn't separate the two events. I kept replaying them in my head and couldn't recapture our love. There was no comfort for me.

Most of the surrounding community wasn't commiserating with my loss. This evoked comparable conditions to when Leon left. Then came September 11th. Everyone was reaching out to their loved ones, wanting closeness during this tragedy. I longed for Leon more than ever. The event was being replayed on every television channel. Then they televised funeral after funeral. The broadcasts kept reminding me of the monumental, missing piece that would forever be absent from Leon's death—a funeral. I got the impression that I was expected to have moved on by now; Leon's death was old news.

13

"Send Me An Angel"

(from Moments of Glory)

by

Scorpions

with Berlin Philharmonic

I was plummeting into the depths of despondency while winter approached. There was a lump in my neck, and swallowing was becoming increasingly painful. Scar tissue from the burns had formed over a salivary gland, blocking it so it became infected. The lump enlarged to the size of a golf ball. I was barely able to eat or drink. Ensure nutritional formula was all I could manage, and even that brought stabbing pain. Consequently, I developed an impacted bowel. I was falling apart physically (I had already fallen apart emotionally). Antibiotics were ineffective. Surgery would be required to cut open my neck for the gland to be excised. The date of the operation was on the exact one-year anniversary of Leon's death.

The medical team needed me to be admitted sooner to try to diminish the swelling prior to surgery so that the risk of nerve damage could be reduced. If nerve damage occurred, half of my face would be paralyzed; nonetheless, there wasn't a choice. The infection was spreading through my system. Antibiotics were administered by IV, and an intravenous catheter (IV PICC line) was ordered to be surgically inserted so they could send me home. When the nurse came into the room after the procedure, she asked who would put the antibiotics into my line. I told her that I lived alone. She said that antibiotics were needed too many times a day for a visiting nurse, so the IV PICC had to then be surgically removed. I wondered why no one had asked me about my living arrangements before the procedure. Needless to say, this added insult to injury regarding Leon being gone and not here to help me.

I was sent home with a prescription for an oral antibiotic to which I'd alerted the medical staff I was allergic. My pharmacist didn't want to fill the order. He called the hospital and was instructed to do so. The surgeon explained it was critical to try to reduce the swelling prior to surgery. He couldn't operate until the swelling went down. I took the antibiotic and got hives all over me. The antibiotic didn't reduce the swelling much, but enough to allow me to have the operation.

When I arrived back at the hospital, they put me in a room with someone who was screaming all day and night while rattling the bed rails. The hospital staff didn't understand that I couldn't have my temperature taken by mouth because of my burns. Every hour, another assistant would come in and try—no matter how hard I tried to explain that it couldn't be done by mouth. In addition, they were angry with me that I couldn't eat the regular food, and they threatened to make me have a feeding tube. My TV didn't work, and no one responded to my inquiry about repairing it. A psychiatrist was sent in without my request. He asked me why I drank Drano when I was a teenager. He even tried to guess. This felt so uncomfortable for me and was unrelated to the surgery itself. With hives, my roommate's screeching, the banging bed rails, and no TV to drown out the noise or my jitters, the night was a waking nightmare.

The next morning on the first anniversary of Leon's death, the gland was excised without nerve damage. Leon's influence must have been in the OR! There were lots of stitches in my neck. I looked like Frankenstein! Physical therapy would be necessary, and only baby food could be eaten for several months. Producing less saliva without the gland would be a permanent result, but there had been no option.

When I got home, I was a basket case. The way I'd been treated at the hospital for surgery to remedy an emergency that was caused by my decades-old suicide attempt reminded me vividly of my previous life in hospitals; plus Leon had now been dead for a year. I followed all of the aftercare protocol, but I didn't feel alive. I was just going through the motions. This continued for months.

When I finally could use my mouth again without excessive pain, I thought perhaps a bereavement support group would be helpful. When

I called around, I was met again with invalidation. I was told that too much time had passed (almost two years at this point). I was also told that I wasn't eligible if my husband and I had divorced. Yikes! I was heartsick. I started asking Leon for help. I begged him to send me an angel.

14

"Sister Seagull"

by

Be Bop Deluxe

I made more calls for grief recovery, but this time I asked for a bereavement counselor instead of a support group. I was given a few names and left messages for them. One didn't have any openings; one was too far away; one had the kindest voice I'd ever heard. Her name was/is Judy. When I met her, I truly thought Leon had sent me an angel. He knew how badly I wanted to heal. He wanted healing for me as badly as I did.

Judy is the personification of compassion. The first thing she taught me about was complicated grief. Yup, that was mine. Then she went on to describe disenfranchised grief, which I'd never heard of and which fit me exactly. It's grief that is not acknowledged by society. How curative it was to learn that an actual category of grief existed which defined my experience! This knowledge felt like manna from heaven. My trust in Judy became unwavering. I shared my core with her. I detailed my fear of invalidation and provided a history of my suicide attempts and hospitalizations. Judy believed that disenfranchised grief also applied to the other significant losses in my life. She expressed her hope that our working through loss would bring me the healing I'd been longing for since youth.

I was wracked with guilt and regret. Judy strove to help me reclaim my relationship with Leon so I'd be able to mourn. The guilt and regret were preventing me from bereavement. She shared with me a passage from A Grief Observed by C.S. Lewis. Its concept of staying in relationship with the deceased resonated with me. I brought Leon's Little Prince notes to our next session so I could share them with Judy. She encouraged me to allow his words to enter my heart and pave the way for reclamation.

On the two-year anniversary of Leon's death, Judy suggested that we have a ceremony to commemorate him. I had some of his ashes. We scattered a portion of them at the ocean, and the rest were kept in a beautiful vase in the condo.

Here's what I said when we scattered the ashes at the ocean:

"*You loved jogging by here each morning as the sun rose.*

And together we treasured our time here.

How I admire your life-loving spirit.

By letting go of these ashes here, may your spirit fill me and anyone else in despair with that same love of life.

May this help me let go of the regret, guilt, and torment that has taken hold of me, and enable me to see my letting you go as an act of love.

Be with the tide, my love, as it moves with such conviction, offering hope for change and the permanence of love that never leaves."

Here's what I said in the condo:

" '*It is only with the heart that one can see rightly; what is essential is invisible to the eye.*'[1]

You wrote that the departure of the body in no way altered love.

This is what it means to see with the heart, you explained.

108

You went on to say that the apparent sad departure is in reality an indication of the maturation of love, in that the common spirit is symbolized by one remaining being.

Simpler put, you said, the departure is a reiteration of the oneness of love—the ultimate maturation of two into one.

I am that remaining being.

I don't understand what has happened, Leni (one of Leon's nicknames).

It feels overwhelming, and I'm suffering.

I miss the you who was with me in the form I recognized on this Earth.

I don't know anything for certain except for this one thing: we loved each other.

That is all I truly know, and I must hold onto this.

I believe we are soulmates, and we are one now.

By placing your ashes here where we lived together, I seek to learn acceptance of what has happened to you, to us, and to me.

May you know that you are accepted as part of me forever.

Let healing find a home here.

May these ashes be a constant reminder that you are still here in some form because love never dies.

'What is essential is invisible to the eye.' "[1]

Here's an excerpt from Judy's speech:

"*Regardless of how much we loved someone, we can still suffer from guilt. We relive, over and over, the mistakes we think we made. Leon's leaving and death have placed self-forgiveness at the center of Amy's healing work.*

I am here today to honor Leon, his humanness, and the love he had for Amy. I am here today to bear witness to the suffering Amy sustains as she makes real Leon's physical absence in her life. I am here to honor Amy for the choice she has made to validate her grief and to acknowledge her love for Leon that has become a part of her healing into herself."

Judy's presence as a witness who knew my story in the unique capacity of grief companion and guide brought perceptible meaning to me. As she had suggested, having some of the ashes and performing a ritual with them did provide the closure

I'd been missing for two years. As we stood together before the serene accepting sea, gratitude became embedded in my soul, like stones in the sand. When Judy picked up a rock from the icy water with her bare hand and gently offered it to me as a tangible keepsake of those moments, the gratitude carried my soul beyond the horizon, as though I, too, were with the tide. The comfort she brought to the ceremony in my home would remain a fixture here. When we looked together at the vase of Leon's ashes, I felt a oneness with her, with Leon, and with the universe.

Even so, the ceremony couldn't quell my regret. I applied my usual technique of doing good deeds in an effort to ward off feeling like a "bad person." In addition to my expansive volunteer work at the synagogue, I was still delivering books to the homebound, as well as participating as an active member of the AIDS Awareness Committee and the Teen Task Force. I'd also assumed more shifts at the Counseling Center and became a mentor at an organization offering support for adults with special needs. The volunteer work had the unintended benefit of providing daily structure, which felt crucial while I was living alone.

15

"Little By Little"

by

Robert Plant

Unfortunately, physical problems caught hold of me again. This time, they were unrelated to my suicide attempt. I had a large, noncancerous tumor compressing my bladder and obstructing my bowel. It had to be removed with extensive abdominal surgery.

Judy accompanied me to the hospital (the same one as where I had my neck cut open). Judy's support gave me the courage to reach out to the surgeon to solicit her understanding and oversight. This surgeon did have compassion for me and for the way I'd been treated before. She furnished her staff with considerate approaches for me.

The anesthesiologist introduced herself to me prior to the operation and shared that she also had decreased saliva. During anesthesia, there was extreme difficulty intubating me because of my scarring. My neck had to be moved in such a way that left me with three herniated disks. The anesthesiologist came into my room after the operation to explain the seriousness of what had occurred and to alert me that I could not be intubated again in the future. She was kind, like the surgeon had been. Their compassion emboldened me to become an advocate for myself.

Judy brought me home from the hospital and came to my condo for our sessions until I recuperated. The regret regarding Leon was still gnawing away at me. When I was able to go back to her office, Judy sensitively expressed to me that she felt I was traumatized—not just from losing Leon, but also from what had happened in my early life. She wanted me to see a trauma specialist to supplement the bereavement counseling. I was terrified by this suggestion. I feared that I'd be invalidated like before—that the trauma specialist would consider my experiences trivial compared to other situations she'd seen. Judy had so much empathy for me that she offered to go with me!

Sandra, the trauma specialist, wasn't like the treatment providers from my past. With Judy by my side, Sandra unhesitatingly and decisively validated me and my experiences. She bestowed upon me the word "trauma" to apply to what had happened in my life. This was a tremendous breakthrough for me. I could see everything through a new lens that brought a clear hope for healing. Judy's compassion and validation, first for my loss of Leon and then for my early life, coupled with Sandra's validation and application of trauma to define my experiences, led me to feel like I had a new lease on life.

Sandra proposed that I create a healing circle. The people in it didn't have to actually be there—just their essence had to be with me. So, of course, I chose Judy and Sandra. I also selected Leon's older sister, Shirley, from Chicago. She was pure love. She'd call several times a week to check on me. If I wasn't home, she'd leave a message that would say, *"It's your sister Shirley calling to say I love you."* (When Shirley died, the circle expanded to include her children and grandchildren.) I taught myself to be surrounded by this circle. I utilized it to help me with my trauma. The compassion and love from Judy, Sandra, and Shirley enabled me to join the circle and feel compassion and love for myself!

Judy came with me to my appointments with Sandra and also saw me individually for bereavement counseling. Judy had been "right on" regarding my being traumatized. We employed the trauma work to devitalize the regret associated with Leon and to subdue the self-reproach. I finally broke free from the loop that perpetually replayed Leon's leaving and dying. I accepted that both the leaving and the dying were traumatic and that both broke my heart. When meeting with Sandra, we did what couldn't be done in the past—focus on my suicide attempts and the underlying issues.

Let's stop for a minute for some affirmation. Leon's death brought me the elements of healing that I'd sought for decades. Now they were being

discovered in a way I'd never imagined possible—
through loss.

PART FOUR

16

"Yesterday To Tomorrow"

by

Audioslave

For years, the three of us (Judy, Sandra, and I) met. We became "dance partners along life's journey." Judy and Sandra were with me when I met my next soulmate, Ben. I'd been going regularly to Sabbath services at my synagogue. One Friday evening, a tall man walking with a cane entered alone and stood by himself during the social gathering that preceded the service. Because of my ardent feelings about inclusion, I approached him. He seemed quite appreciative to have someone greet him. He shared with me that his wife had died not too long ago. I told him about Leon. He dolefully said that he was too old to ever have another relationship. We then went into the sanctuary for the service. The next day, I thought it would be kind to check in with him. When I called, I felt a sort of electricity run through my fingers and said aloud to myself, "*This is going to change my life*." I don't know how I knew!

Ben immediately recognized my voice on the phone. He thanked me for calling. He then said, "*I have feelings, you know.*" I asked what he meant. He explained that he was told it was weak for a man to have feelings, but he had them and wanted to be free to release them. I exclaimed, "*You've sure come to the right place!*"

That evening we got together. We openly learned about one another. He was 40 years older than I, yet we felt like kindred spirits. I disclosed what I'd done to myself. He listened lovingly. He sheepishly confided that he had to wear a pad because he'd had prostate cancer. I replied that the pad went wonderfully with the bib I had to wear when I ate because of my scarring and my difficulty with swallowing.

The next time we got together, Ben brought two matching bibs—one for each of us. He related that he mentioned going out with me to some people, and they interrogated him about whether he knew what I'd done to myself. He retorted that I'd divulged this information to him right away. He then defended me by asserting to them, "*From the ashes rose a phoenix.*" At that instant, I knew we were soulmates.

Ben presented me with a poem he'd written:

Is I was
Was I am
Now I saw the sun rise
Who are you? Who sent you? Did you hear me?
I'm so excited
For I know because of you
I will be more than I am
I will be exposed to the sun
And now I know I will not wait for the sunset

Oh, I was so deeply moved. I wrote a reply to his poem:

Is I was
Was I am
I saw only the sunset
You heard me in the darkness
I'm so grateful
For I know because of you
I will be more than I am
I will be exposed to the light
And now I know in my heart I will feel the sunrise

We'd both lost our mates and possessed an abiding gratitude for our connection. Ben proclaimed that we'd heard each other's song. We lived each day to the fullest extent. Guess what...He loved playing games! He taught me his favorite: Rummy-Cube. I'd never played it before. It was fantastic and made us use our brains! Ben kept the tiles out on the table in the den, so we could easily start a game at any time. I'd come over after my workday. I'd stay until he went to sleep, and then I'd head home to take care of my clients' tasks and my household chores.

Ben came with me when I went to my clients. We'd take advantage of being in the city and partake in recreational diversions while there, such as a Swan Boat ride or a Duck Tour. Just as Leon had written me a note each morning, I'd write Ben a note each night when he went to bed to greet him in the morning by delineating our day together. The notes captured the gist of our relationship. Here's an example for you:

Duck Tour

"Good Morning Plucky,

Thank you for a spectacular day yesterday.

We went on the Duck Tour together! We did it! You were absolutely fabulous. You wore your captain's hat and yellow duck sunglasses. I thought they were going to make you the guide!

The sun was glistening, and the air was crisp and clear. It was fun seeing some of the famous architecture in Boston. The State House was gorgeous with that golden dome. Boston Commons looked so beautiful.

My favorite part of the trip was when we went into the Charles River. I've driven by it so many times, always longing to be on it. It truly was thrilling. Your little binoculars were fun. What a good idea! The water, sky, views of Boston's buildings and bridges were phenomenal from the Charles River.

I adored it with you, babe! Thanks for making the enormous effort. How could I ask for a better day? I love being with you!

Love,

Quacky"

Ben would write back to me on the note itself:

"I've begun to have a full life with love, kindness, and respect. The sun is shining. I'm out in the world, filled with laughter, and grateful for these days. Every day is a thrill being with you. You make it happen with happiness. I love you."

17

"Adventure of a Lifetime"

by

Coldplay

Ben and I enjoyed movies, plays, festivals, BINGO, amusement parks, symphony, miniature golf, and we even attended Cirque du Soleil! I brought him to a session with Judy and Sandra so they could all meet. Ben and I cherished each other and our expeditions. Every single second was appreciated by both of us.

Then Ben found out that his aortic valve was narrowing, and open heart surgery was required to replace it. I was faced with another soulmate in need of heart valve surgery, but this time I could be by my loved one's side. Both of us felt blessed to be with each other.

The medical care became quite intensive. I chose to learn as much as possible and to be Ben's caregiver. In order to do this plus continue to service my clients, it was necessary for me to give up all my volunteer positions except the synagogue. Sandra admired my caregiving so much that she decided it was time to close her practice and move out-of-state to care for her relatives. She continued to have sessions with me over the phone, and eventually we stayed in each other's lives as dear friends and soulmates. I don't think I could've cared for Ben so thoroughly and lovingly without her and Judy's steadfast support.

I don't want to overload you with medical details, so I'll try to summarize. The aortic valve replacement was successful, but there were many complications. Fluid collapsed one of Ben's lungs, and he then had to undergo open chest surgery with drainage tubes. This led to pneumonia and GI bleeding necessitating blood transfusions and cauterization. He was moved from the ICU to a hospital room, then to rehab for a long period of time. I brought Rummy-Cube for us to play there. He taught me a fun card game called Casino, which we could deal on the little bedside table. We stayed in life.

Upon discharge, it was recommended that Ben use a walker. I got him a fancy one with brakes and a seat. We walked short distances in the condo hallways with it so he could build back some strength. His effort was awe-inspiring.

When he was strong enough to begin going outdoors again, I took him to scenic spots where we could play some games and also simply be in the moment together with our love for each other. Our favorite venue was the lighthouse. We talked about everything under the sun. We discussed marriage, but I thought it would make things harder for his children. We decided to have a commitment ceremony with my bereavement counselor, Judy, officiating. Here's the note I wrote to him afterwards:

"*Good morning my love to whom I am bonded!*

Thank you for yesterday! It was bliss—truly perfect from start to finish. We've been blessed, and we know it. Even the way the day started off so gloomy and stormy and then brightened up just at the right time was a blessing and a metaphor for our lives. And it gave us glorious scenery without many people.

I loved helping you get dressed in that dashing outfit. You looked incredibly handsome. We coordinated our color scheme. It was uncanny how Judy matched us!

Picking out the flowers for Judy was fun. The delicate roses were beautiful. Thanks for getting a bouquet for me too!

Judy had a parking space saved for us. She prepared a meaningful speech and read us a thought-provoking poem about love.

It was a most tender moment when we placed the 'ring-a-dings' on each other's fingers. They are elegant in their simplicity. I am proud to be wearing them together—and of what they represent.

Judy seemed to appreciate the flowers and gift certificate. She brought us flowers too and an exquisite clear heart. As you so eloquently stated, her presence was the real gift.

Then we went to Temple—where we met one year ago. The sermon was about the heart—just like our day!

I will treasure this day (and all our days together) for as long as I live.

THANK YOU! Your love to whom you are bonded."

Ben wrote:

"Never have I had such love as you have given me. I love you sincerely and deeply. You must have come from HEAVEN. You are my life, my love. I love, I trust, I care. I want to cry."

We dressed up for Halloween as "Prisoners of Love." I wore a convict uniform, and Ben wore a badge and prison warden cap as the guard who captured me. We lived with gusto until Ben developed pleural effusion in his other lung and had to have surgery with chest tubes again. Multiple blood transfusions were administered. Due to his lengthy hospital stays, he was exposed to infection. Sadly, Ben got Clostridium difficile. This was problematic because it was highly contagious. Ben was immensely appreciative of my care. One of his little scrawls on my daily notes was:

"Thank you for so much. I can't count the things you do. Even clean floors, etc., etc."

After another long admission, he was discharged with the instructions to use a wheelchair and oxygen. I got him a comfortable, folding wheelchair that fit in my car. We learned how to obtain and utilize the oxygen. After a while, we were back in action! Even though he thought he looked like Gunga Din, I called him Superman. We went to a wedding together. When it came time to dance, he asked me to lift him from his wheelchair. He held onto the tent pole and shimmied. This gave new meaning to pole dancing! We drove home with the moonroof open, and Ben marveled at the stars. There was a sense of timelessness with us.

18

"Thank You"

by

Led Zeppelin

The next major setback came when Ben developed kidney failure. He had to go on dialysis three times per week. Each treatment lasted for about four hours. I tried to make the time pass for him in a more entertaining way by getting a portable DVD player and inserting his favorite Westerns. Then he needed a pacemaker. What a trooper! He never complained and always adhered to whatever protocol, dietary restriction, exercise regimen, medication, or procedure was advised. We lived life in a sacred space that bordered death. This place provided us with the mindfulness to be in the present moment with gratitude.

After dialysis on a late summer day, I took Ben to a picturesque park overlooking the harbor. I brought a compact folding table and chair. Ben sat in his wheelchair with his oxygen. We were playing cards when a hedgehog scampered out from under a bush and perched itself next to Ben. Usually these animals are nocturnal, so we were surprised. The critter wouldn't leave Ben. Curious children came over and tried to distract the little creature. It wouldn't budge. Ben softly remarked, "*The hedgehog knows I'm gonna die soon.*"

When he got an infection at dialysis, Ben's system began to shut down. He was admitted to hospice, and dialysis was stopped. This meant that death would soon follow. Judy and Sandra were my rocks. I brought Ben all the foods he'd had to stop eating when on dialysis and cardiac care. We played games and watched shows until he was too weak. The last words he spoke were, "*I'll never forget the lighthouse.*" Then he went into a deep slumber.

I was instructed to go home and get some rest. I'd be contacted when I should return. When the nurse called to alert me that death was imminent, I wore my lighthouse T-shirt to the nursing home. When the nurse walked in, she was wearing a pendant. I never notice jewelry, but this shining charm caught my attention. I asked her what it was. She answered that it was a lighthouse. I was moved to tears and reached for Ben. He died holding my hand.

There was a funeral. Rabbi gave me a black ribbon to wear. I wasn't sure whether I'd be allowed, since Ben and I weren't legally married. Phew! I was thankful and recognized the significance of the ritual. Rabbi also invited me to write a eulogy, which he read at the service. This meant the world to me. Here's an excerpt from what I wrote:

"Gratitude was our guide as Ben and I lived life to its fullest, even while the threat of death shared our path. Never have I witnessed a human being try as hard to live. Ben endured so much, yet was willing to adhere to every restriction and regimen.

This gentle man's fortitude was awe-inspiring. Even when his body was weak, he offered the strength of his love to everyone around him. I never met anyone with such a generous capacity to give love.

How I admire Ben's wonderful sense of humor and his compassion, warmth, and depth of emotion. Ben truly listened and wanted to understand. He has taught me how to open up to life and be present with a clear heart.

Together we shared an awareness of the gift of each moment, appreciating laughter and play as each other's best friend and soulmate...from Swan Boat rides and Duck Tours to Rummy-Cube and Casino; from theater, symphony, and movies to sunrises, sunsets, and stars.

It may have appeared that I was a caregiver for Ben as he underwent many medical challenges, but it was his care for me that gave me life. Our relationship was like a lighthouse...providing us with safety, steadfast companionship, and a beacon to show us the way. Ben will always be my guiding light, my love, my life."

Judy came to the funeral. She also made a donation to hospice in memory of Ben. Here's the wording from the letter she attached:

"Please accept this donation in memory of Benjamin Harsip who died on September 30 of this year under the care of your hospice. Please accept this donation in the name of his life partner, Amy Saltz.

If ever there were an angel walking among us, Amy would be that embodiment. Ben was given over to your care from hers. Her care of him was a practice in love, courage, and immense physical and mental stamina.

You walked in her footsteps, and I thank you for helping Ben and Amy at the end of Ben's life."

I felt exceedingly honored by Judy's gesture and her words!

I got a leaf on the Temple's Tree of Life in memory of Ben:

IN LOVING MEMORY OF BENJAMIN HARSIP

WITH HEARTFELT GRATITUDE

BY AMY SALTZ

There were many poignant facets of my relationship with Ben that brought me healing. As rigorous as the caregiving was, every instant brought me what I'd longed to have been able to do for Leon. It felt akin to a do-over. The blessed way Ben and I lived and loved was restorative for me. Carpe diem (seize the day) was our motto! Leon had arrived at that axiom with his surgery, but then he tragically died—and I wasn't physically by his side. Ben's dying while holding my hand was a most precious gift. From no funeral for Leon to a funeral for Ben in which I could participate—this was a discernible amelioration. Just like I thought Leon sent Judy to me, I felt Ben was sent to me also. I had no regrets this time around and could readily embark on bereavement. The marked differences between the circumstances surrounding the two deaths brought me clarity and compassion for my regret regarding Leon. They also served as a resolute reminder of the vast reaches of Leon's hope for my healing.

PART FIVE

19

"Let It Grow"

by

Eric Clapton

It took some time for me to regroup and catch up with myself after the years of strenuous caregiving for Ben. There was a noticeable vacancy in my routine, but my clients' work, volunteering at the synagogue, and rest filled it for a while. Then I signed up for djembe drum lessons at the center where I'd taken Ben for physical therapy. The rhythms energized me. I sent away for a variety of other percussion instruments to learn online. Bopping was enlivening! I was inspired to put my music collection, which had been comprised of vinyl record albums, cassette tapes, and CDs, onto an iPod. This enterprise assembled the musical composition of my life and was exhilarating.

After Ben died, I seemed to possess a newfound eagerness for connection. My dear friend, Sandy, had an idea. She knew how much I loved games and imagined I'd be missing playing them with Ben. She took me under her wing and taught me the complex game of Mah Jongg. I'd never played it before, but I admired the artistic tiles, the eloquent symbolism based on the I Ching and Tai Chi, and the way it encouraged fully immersed concentration. I became absorbed and enraptured with Mah Jongg. It represented a way to make the most out of what's been dealt. It felt like a metaphor for life! In addition, it was the ultimate way to connect. Sandy welcomed me into her group. We'd spend hours playing, focusing on our tiles while cultivating our friendships.

The game felt so therapeutic to me that I started a Mah Jongg program at the synagogue— open to all levels, with lessons for beginners, and tables configured by players' pace. I taught many— the youngest was 7, and the oldest was 91! Several who came to learn were recently widowed. They shared with me that this was their safe place, and they looked forward to coming. Every week I'd email over 70 players and await their replies so I could know how many tables to set up. Their messages were cordial and appreciative. They also kept me apprised of important events in their lives as well as ways I could help them feel more comfortable. My heart felt full when I'd scan the room filled with multiple tables of people connecting with one another. I was putting my whole self in, and the effort was yielding something that felt to me like Tikkun Olam (repairing the world).

I held the belief that healing could blossom and flourish with just about any human interaction involving connection. No activity was any more or less important than another. They all had the potential to effectuate healing. If I offered accessibility, appreciation, kindness, inclusion, validation, and compassion (the attributes I'd sought for healing), participants would feel safe, accepted, and loved. Maybe they'd then be able to pass the love along. It seemed that so much was out of our control; but the way we treat others felt within our control. We could treat people with friendly kindness. We could extend a gentle smile. Eureka! I was no longer doing the volunteer work to offset my feeling like a "bad person!" Plus I was feeling deeply connected with people versus sustaining acute dissociation. I'd found community in the same town where for years I'd felt ostracized.

The synagogue was like a second home to me, and the people there were like family. What a blessing! Throughout Ben's illnesses and dying, I continued to do the projects that Judith had presented to me years ago. Those tasks were all done as an individual. Now I was branching out to organize activities with groups of people. This was a milestone for me!

In addition to the weekly Mah Jongg program, I initiated a monthly Movie Night open to all. I learned how to run the projector and sound system. I researched websites and read reviews in order to select informative and clever films. I'd supply popcorn and candy for the evening of entertainment. Without my ever asking, folks began to bring cookies, cakes, and fruit. Several times, dinner was served before the films. I got speakers to come as well. Attendees expressed interest in the film topics and thankfulness for the welcoming nature of the program.

So now there were two M's: Mah Jongg and Movie Night. I made it 3M when I became the chairperson of the Music Neighborhood—open to all ages and musical abilities to sing together for joy rather than for performance. With an inclusive music specialist directing us on guitar, a keyboardist, a violinist, a clarinetist, and yours truly as percussionist, we were exuberantly rockin'! I could feel Leon and Ben at the Music Neighborhood gatherings. Our group arranged some unique gigs at nursing homes and rehab facilities. We also participated in the Community Holocaust Commemoration. Once we conducted a "Sing-In" for members of all local houses of worship to unite with songs of peace from the 1960s and 1970s. Whenever the Music Neighborhood sang together, we felt our souls were being filled. My 3M activities (Mah Jongg, Movie Night, and Music Neighborhood) were bolstering my healing in a most marvelous manner.

20

"We Used To Know"

by

Jethro Tull

At this point in time, something that seemed disadvantageous turned out to change my life in an unexpectedly constructive and profound way. Some physiological symptoms led to a biopsy confirming that I have small fiber polyneuropathy. My PCP referred me to a physician named Harvey who helps people with physiological symptoms that no other doctors treat. He tries to see the whole person and sits with the patient while an entire history is recounted.

After hearing about Leon, Harvey gave me the piece that was missing from my healing. He taught me about traumatic brain injury. This is what Leon was suffering from. Leon's behavior was out of his control. If we'd known this when he was alive, he wouldn't have felt such shame and the need to leave, and I would've been able to work with him as a teammate. How I wish we'd known then! I wouldn't have wondered whether I was in an abusive relationship. This aspect had affected me in a deleterious way. Leon was so loving, kind, and respectful until those frightening episodes that were completely out of character occurred. I could never reconcile the behavior nor the way I stayed with it. Now that I'd been given an explanation that made absolute sense, I was able to find understanding and forgiveness for both of us. I could finally affirm that Leon hadn't ever left me. He'd been with me all along, and he'd be with me forevermore.

Not long after receiving this vital information about Leon, a storm with blustery winds caused a large limb of the tree next to Leon's memorial bench at the park to break off and smash the bench. Both the tree and the bench were removed. When I called the Park Department, I ascertained that the plaque had been salvaged. When I went to pick it up, I inquired about having the bench replaced. They told me that the warranty had expired. It was very expensive to purchase a new one. The price had tripled since Leon died. They proposed rebuilding the bench using the broken pieces. I replied that I loved that idea. That was my life! When I sat on the "new" old bench after it was installed, I could see and feel our joy. After years of working to understand what happened with Leon, I'd reached peace for both of us. I was transmitting information about traumatic brain injury to him so we could both shed any shame. His death was a tragedy, but I could now separate that from his leaving. The bench held all the broken pieces with love.

Harvey gave me another gift. He asked if I'd like to present at Schwartz Rounds, which are hospital seminars to increase compassion and more meaningful collaboration between patients and medical professionals. What an honor! How gratifying it felt to be asked to share my experiences in order to help others. My topic was about having compassion for people who attempt suicide. Here are some of the key points I was able to disseminate (I've already shared most of these with you, but now you'll have them in one spot.):

SOME KEY POINTS:

As an adult, I hold firmly to the belief that we can recover emotionally from just about anything if we're treated with compassion and given validation.

As a youth in my early teens, I reached out for help. For reasons unknown to me, I was repeatedly invalidated. The invalidation caused my emotional pain to intensify and become accompanied by deep shame.

I felt alone and disconnected from the people and the world around me. A metaphor that comes close to the feeling I had is that of an astronaut whose lifeline has been severed and is dangling in the dark void of space. Something frightening was happening to me. I didn't feel safe in this world. The actions that followed did not feel like a choice. At the time, they seemed to be the only way to safety.

My life learning has taught me that suicide or self-destructive behavior is not a choice. Lack of clarity about this may be where some of the judgment that blocks compassion for those who have attempted suicide resides. Patients are blamed and judged as if they had made a conscious choice with clear minds. This wasn't the case for me, and I don't think it is in general.

What the adolescent Amy did that took only a few seconds, the adult Amy lives with for a lifetime. To this day, when I share what happened with new medical personnel, I am often viewed as a mentally-ill individual, even though the event occurred over 40 years ago. Also in the present day, when seeking treatment for medical issues caused by the event, I sometimes feel judged for what I'd done as an adolescent and held responsible for the current consequences.

I've worked hard with my present treatment providers and feel we've established mutual respect and regard for each other.

We work together as a team. I think they've even utilized me to deepen their understanding of patient needs.

I had always sought healing, but unfortunately was harmed in the process when I was young. It wasn't until decades later, after my husband died, when I found a bereavement counselor to help me with this loss, that I was given the opportunity to share all of the other losses with an enlightened witness. The bereavement counselor truly heard me and validated me with undying compassion and without judgment; she gave me life. She has helped me understand trauma; this word being applied to my experiences was a breakthrough for me—the ultimate validation and corroboration that my actions were not chosen. Prior to this, I couldn't let go of self-blame for the tragic mistake I'd made. I've been learning to validate my experiences internally rather than seeking validation from external sources. This is still a work in progress.

I think the feeling of being disconnected is what can lead a person to suicide. The alienation and isolation associated with feeling disconnected can be catastrophic. If there could be the feeling of connection with just one other person or a pet or even a hobby, the suffering individual would be tethered to some aspect of life. To me, the sense of connection is the antidote to hopelessness; with it can come meaning, joy, and gratitude (even with loss).

Whatever reason a person gives for attempting suicide, that reason caused enough suffering to provoke that action. What matters is the suffering, not whether the reason given seems significant enough to another person. It is important that the individual is helped to understand why the suicidal feelings exist, but the reason is valid no matter what it is. I think it's the emotional impact of whatever is being experienced that causes a person to feel suicidal, and this is where compassion and validation can intervene for healing.

Presenting at Schwartz Rounds was such a momentous occurrence for me that I wrote about it right when I got home so I'd not forget the details:

I was ready. I'd written a speech that would take about ten minutes to read. Imagine encapsulating a lifetime into a blip. It actually can be done! I awoke a minute before the alarm was about to ring. Harvey called to check on me. He could sense nervousness. Yes, I was anxious, but I was also brimming with willingness. Before I headed out, I said a little prayer to Leon asking him to be at the hospital with me.

It was a glorious autumn day. The light was gentle. As I approached the hospital, my heart skipped a beat. I hadn't been in that area since I attempted suicide there. After parking my car, I got out and walked to the spot where it had happened. Miraculous peace came over me. Here I was, alive and being asked to share my experience—to be heard...and I could speak after years of not being able to do so. Immeasurable gratitude permeated my being.

As I walked toward the entry, I was greeted by Harvey. He introduced me to his colleagues and invited me to sit at the table with him. I was struck by the contrast between this treatment and that of the young girl who was an inpatient decades ago. It didn't seem real. Again, gratitude welled up within me.

The sun magnificently streamed into the room. At first there weren't many people in attendance, so my nervousness seemed to abate. Judy came in, and that helped as well. Then lots of people entered and more were on their way. There weren't any empty seats. It was happening. I was reading my notes to this room filled with nurses, social workers, doctors, and students.

When I finished speaking, there was dead silence. Oh no! Then one kind woman Harvey had introduced to me asked a wonderful question. One question sparked another and another. Oh yes! I tried to engage with each person who had the courage to participate. Not only did they ask thoughtful questions, many shared personally. This touched me deeply. I hope I gave something of myself and my experience that can help them with their patients.

After the discussion, several attendees approached me. One was a speech therapist who empathized with my efforts to teach myself how to talk, swallow, and eat. Another was a student who told me that my story changed her life. A nurse came up to me and said she wanted to apologize to me for the medical profession. Then a social worker told me she'd been a bit distracted because a cardinal had been at the window behind me. I was already amazed by the day, but this brought it to another level. After Leon died, his sister Shirley in Chicago caringly called me every week. She loved me unconditionally. When she died several years ago, a cardinal kept coming to the window. Her kids associated the cardinal with Shirley. Now the cardinal was at the window during Schwartz Rounds. Leon heard my prayer! He wanted me to find healing, and his death is what brought it to me. I am in the presence of healers—Judy, Sandra, and now Harvey. May I contribute in whatever way I am asked with an open, grateful spirit.

I was asked to present at Schwartz Rounds at another hospital, where I was later invited to teach some classes for a psychology training program. Soon thereafter, Harvey arranged for me to present a seminar for psychiatry residents at a medical school. Who would've believed this could ever happen? For so many years, I'd felt "less than" because I didn't have any college degrees— especially when I'd been the top student, destined to become a psychologist. Now I was harnessing my life's education, and its merits were valued. I knew I was blessed again with a compassionate soul (Harvey) who cared about my very being.

Since losing Leon, I'd been avidly riding my bike. I was known as the "wicked witch of the North Shore." I always wore a helmet and reflective gear. My bike had lights on the front and back with tires that glowed in the dark. These safety measures were of no help when in broad daylight the door of a parked car opened into me, slamming me onto the ground. I was unconscious for hours. I awoke in the ER with a concussion. I followed medical advice for concussion care at home, but weeks later was still sustaining a chemical depression. Since childhood, I'd grappled with depression. Because of my extensive oral injuries, I couldn't take antidepressants due to the dry mouth side-effect. I'd forced myself to accept depression and to fight for life. The post-concussive depression was much worse than I'd ever encountered. I didn't know how I'd persist.

Harvey and I did some research together and found a wearable neurostimulation device that helps the brain produce serotonin, dopamine, and beta-endorphin, while it lowers the cortisol stress hormone. It's called the Fisher Wallace Stimulator, and it changed my life. I must never have had the proper amount of serotonin in my brain before using this mechanism because I was always trapped in gloom. After two weeks of use, the neurostimulator lifted me out of the doldrums and permitted perspective. This battery-operated implement delivers a gentle electrical stimulus via wires with wet sponges that are placed on the temple areas of the head under a Velcro band. It's recommended to be used twice a day for twenty minutes. It has a clip, so it can be worn while doing activities. It doesn't have side effects. Before using this device, it was a battle to brave the day. Now I felt part of life.

21

"Titan"

by

Phideaux

Judy had been planning her retirement and had already closed her private practice. I was her last remaining client. The bike accident had prolonged our termination date. With my depression allayed, we planned our final session. It would be held at the seashore where we scattered Leon's ashes. We'd collect rocks from the beach and write some chosen words on them with indelible ink. Then we'd toss them into the ocean for Leon. Here were the words we selected:

UNABLE	ACKNOWLEDGMENT
SACRED WORK	HEALING
LIGHT	LOVE
ESSENCE	ONENESS
SOULMATES	TOGETHER
GRATITUDE	THANKS

Here's what I said after we threw our stones into the water:

"*This anniversary of your death was my last one while working with Judy. She has been a healing godsend to me.*

In our work with Sandra and Harvey, we have learned about the impact of your brain injury. It wasn't that you were unwilling to try to work on certain behavioral issues—you were unable. Sadly, we didn't know this during your time on Earth, and then you died so tragically. I am doing my best to convey this to you spiritually along with the acknowledgment I don't think you received enough of when you were alive.

You found me, taught me about love and light, and gave me a home and a profession. You cared for both grandmothers with dedication. You always wanted me to heal, and because of you I have been given the opportunity to do so with Judy.

Part of <u>my</u> healing is <u>your</u> healing because we're soulmates. We (both Leon and I) thank Judy with our deepest gratitude and love."

I got another leaf on the Temple's Tree of Life and created a handmade replica for Judy to keep on her desk:

IN DEEP APPRECIATION FOR

THE WORK OF LOVE AND HEALING

BROUGHT TO

AMY SALTZ

BY JUDY SEIFERT

AND LEON WISEL

Like Sandra, Judy has stayed in my life as a dear friend and soulmate. She has been the closest person to me.

Could I possibly find another partner? The way people were doing it now was online. I compiled a profile. As a non-gendered individual in my fifties with an intricate history, I wasn't optimistic. A woman my age from the town next to mine responded. I told her the tough stuff. Patty wanted to give me a chance. She tried to learn about my limitations. I tried to do the same with hers. Even though mine were less common, we determined that everyone had some. Each of us had adjusted to living on our own and appreciated our independence. We both enjoyed movies, plays, concerts, walking along the seashore, kayaking, mini-pong, pool, Wii, coloring, gazing at the sky, and yes—playing games! We formed a partnership that included her lovable dog. About a year and a half later, Judy officiated a commitment ceremony for us at the lighthouse. We exchanged rings depicting ocean waves with sunlight glistening on them.

22

"Horizon"

by

Steve Winwood

I longed to do something to acknowledge Judy, Sandra, and Harvey while they were alive, as well as to provide some hope to anyone who'd experienced loss. One of the tools I utilized with the bereavement counselor and trauma specialist was writing. I began writing a story about Leon's death and put it aside when I met Ben. I picked up the story again after Ben died, then put it back in the folder. When Judy retired, I picked up the story again to bring it to fruition. Then it went back in the folder.

After I presented at Schwartz Rounds, Harvey encouraged me to write a book about my experiences. He gave me an assignment—one paragraph for our next session. I tried and tried and crumpled up so many sheets of paper. Feeling like a failure, I didn't want to go empty-handed, so I thought to bring my story from the folder. I explained to Harvey what happened and read the story I brought. We both cried. He said this was what to publish! I agreed. This metaphorical story wouldn't hurt anyone. And after reading it this time,

I saw that I really had found healing. I was overcome with gratitude and a desire to offer thanks. I hired an illustrator, Patty typed and edited, and the story became a published book entitled <u>An Essential Song</u>.

I'd met the illustrator at the synagogue. My own experience of living with handicaps prompted me to embrace Mike's attentive allegiance to the project even though he couldn't see color. We devised a method to visually communicate. The illustrations were beyond expectation and represented the triumph of the human spirit. The illustrator had painted vividly colorful renditions without the ability to see color, and the author (I) was singing <u>An Essential Song</u> without a full tongue!

The book that had meant the most to me throughout my life was <u>The Little Prince</u>. The quotation upon which Leon and I based our relationship was, "*It is only with the heart that one can see rightly; what is essential is invisible to the eye.*"[1] It was thrilling to receive permission from Antoine de Saint-Exupery's publisher to include this quotation in my book's preface. I chose the word "essential" to be part of my book's title. The philosophical notes Leon wrote while reading <u>The Little Prince</u> revealed that he had understood an essential song before I even grasped the concept! Ben understood all along. When we first met he declared, "*We heard each other's song. Together we sing!*"

In <u>An Essential Song</u>, there is a fisherman. The fisherman represents whoever or whatever brings hope and healing to each individual. For me, the fisherman started as a combination of Judy, Sandra, and Harvey—the embodiment of the quest for healing. It was my way of thanking them for the healing they made possible for me. As I healed, the fisherman became a part of me—like the song. When I sing, I am connected to spirit. There isn't a moment that passes that I don't appreciate the miracle of being able to sing (regardless of whether or not I have a melodious voice). Plus, I've been blessed with soulmates, including my present-day partner, Patty, who fully accepts me. When I look at what tragedy brought me and witness the depth of compassion, it feels sacred. I can see it as coming from God or being God. I wish for all of us to be able to express our losses—any and all kinds of losses, emotions, and experiences—and find healing.

A book launch was held at the Temple. I figured we could have it in the Library and sit around the conference table. The office staff suggested that we conduct it in the Fellowship Room. I thought that would be too large a space to fill. As the hour approached, people were piling in. The Fellowship Room was overcrowded! We moved into the Sanctuary. I was overcome with boundless appreciation for the magnanimous show of support.

An Essential Song won some awards that boosted my confidence:

2018 Living Now Bronze Award Winner for Grieving/Death & Dying

2019 Montaigne Medal Finalist

2019 First Horizon Award Finalist

2019 National Indie Excellence Award Finalist for Grief

2019 Eric Hoffer Award Honorable Mention Winner for Spiritual

This recognition gave me the courage to write FINDING THE SONG: Living After Attempting Suicide, which is the comprehensive, nonfiction version of An Essential Song.

23

"Universal"

by

Anathema

While receiving the remarkable attention for my published book, I had another health scare related to the suicide attempt. A CT scan had detected a growth in the gland on the opposite side from the one that had required excision. I'd been living with the new growth and applying meticulous self-care to the area. In spite of my assiduous efforts, a lump was forming on that side of my neck. Now I couldn't be intubated, so how would surgery be performed? Would this be my end? I made an appointment at the hospital with the surgeon. Patty accompanied me. Fortunately, the gland wasn't infected, and the swelling subsided. The growth is still there, and it presents a continuously looming threat for me.

I decided to take care of some end-of-life matters while I was capable. I established <u>FINDING THE SONG: Restricted Fund For Suicidal Individuals</u> at the Marblehead Counseling Center (66 Clifton Avenue in Marblehead, MA 01945). This would be my legacy. I updated my will and purchased a prepaid funeral plan. Judy and Patty came with me to the funeral home and were designated as my agents.

There were lots of decisions to be made and forms to finalize. I was able to complete most of the forms there—except for the pre-composed obituary. Yuck! I asked Judy to help me write this. She came over a few weeks later. We took a walk first and stopped in at a ceramic studio that I knew she'd relish. Our friendship was broadening. We'd even gone to see Lily Tomlin with Patty! When we got back to my home, we sat on the deck where Leon and I used to play. Judy and I both observed the awesomeness of our being there together. We called Sandra, and the three of us linked lovingly. We were ebulliently in step with one another. After the call, Judy and I commenced with brainstorming about the obituary. I took copious notes.

When Judy left, we set up a time for me to call her with a rough draft. When I called Judy at our agreed-upon time, she shared with me some shocking news. She had just received a diagnosis of stage 4 esophageal cancer. I was thunderstruck. Here she was helping me with my preplanned obituary! I had to totally regroup. Now it would be my turn to be here for Judy. My empathy was overflowing. Judy's diagnosis has opened to her some of the same challenges that I have faced with swallowing, eating, pain, and trauma. We've felt and learned from each other's presence every step of the way. Our work has been transcendent.

Sandra's mother died shortly after Judy received her diagnosis. Now I would be holding both Judy and Sandra as the three of us did our life dance. Even if our dance on Earth ended, grace would be with us. Our harmony would carry us eternally. The synagogue, my volunteer activities, and work with clients would keep the beat of my daily life. Harvey would be my bridge to resolution, where the dissonance of my past could progress to consonance and inner peace. He'd also help me to vocalize my story. Leon, Ben, and Patty would always compose the notes to serenade my heart. I was whole. I'd found the song.

Epilogue

"Oneness"

by

Carlos Santana

(instrumental)

Leon and I used to visit my ailing grandmother at the nursing home on a regular basis. I told Leon that I wouldn't want to wind up in a place like that. He said that he wouldn't mind being there because he could still have his music. He had something that I didn't have back then—gratitude for what is here in the moment. He recognized that music is a life force to hold us and to behold. He knew its amazing capacity to unite with the soul. Ben had the very same awareness.

As I trace my pursuit of healing in the context of my relationship with music, I am awestruck by the way music has reached me. Almost everything I've learned can be expressed by sharing how it became actualized through music.

During my youth and adolescence, I used my music to insulate myself from the world around me. I gravitated towards psychedelic, hard, and progressive rock. These genres sounded the way I felt, with their winding guitar distortion. Their lyrics spoke to me. They shared my depression, shame, and hell, and they were philosophical. I connected with this music as if it were a nonjudgmental friend, and I let out my emotions with it.

I missed my music very much while hospitalized, but I never forgot it. It hibernated within me, awaiting its awakening. When I was in the halfway house and was finally able to have audio equipment in my room, the music was revived. It was a song that helped me get through the stigmatization I was experiencing after being in mental hospitals for so long. "Creative compensation" was in force. I was learning in ways that worked for me—without a classroom or textbooks, but with song lyrics!

It was because of music that I met Leon. We bonded over his singing reggae while jogging. That day was the first time I'd ever felt gratitude—and the sunshine. The musical genres I was drawn to expanded to include reggae, funk, rhythm and blues, alternative, indie, acoustic, and love songs! Music facilitated our opening ourselves to human love. We danced with unmitigated joy.

Music and dancing were integral components of our married life. Songs connected us when Leon left. He played and replayed the CD of his favorite songs I'd sent him for his birthday. When his belongings were returned to me after he died and I found the CD, I played it over and over again. Then I made a new CD that combined the songs with his voice mail messages. The songs coupled with his voice were the instrument I used to unlock my grief. It was one of the songs (Send Me An Angel), which I sang while sobbing, that I believe prompted Leon to send me Judy.

When Judy taught me about disenfranchised grief regarding Leon's death and the other losses I'd experienced, I began the process of reclamation. When Judy accompanied me to meet with Sandra, and "trauma" was applied to define my experiences,

I was able to start to heal after so many years of yearning to do so. For the first time, I could listen to Leon's songs and remember our dancing together...without feeling regret. Judy, Sandra, and I called ourselves "dance partners along life's journey."

When I met Ben, he professed that we met because we heard each other's song. Our life together was like a concert. Judy and Sandra were my rocks while I cared for Ben and when he died. Ben's dying while holding my hand brought me the solace that welcomed unhindered bereavement—the ability to just simply grieve. As with Leon's death, music played an important role. This time, I literally used the hand that held Ben's...to play the djembe drum and pick up a practice of percussion. It reminded me of the heartbeat. I was connecting with music in a hands-on manner, which instilled within me the confidence and desire to amplify my associations by chairing a musical collective. Whenever our group sang together, our spirits soared. I was putting my whole self in, and it was turning me around—from mourning to jubilation.

When I consolidated my music collection onto an iPod, the miracle of healing evidenced itself. Lots of the songs had been on vinyl record albums and cassette tapes that weren't easy to access on up-to-date audio systems, so I hadn't heard them in decades. Now I could listen and distinctly remember how I felt when I first heard them. I could compare myself now with myself then. What a transformation! (Reminder: The only person to ever compare yourself with is yourself, okay?) I overflowed with thankfulness for what music had given me. As a young person, it enabled me to feel my emotions instead of bottling them up. I had replayed the songs that echoed what I was going through so I could try to process what was happening within and around me. As an adult, I could see quite clearly that my adolescent self truly had been trying to survive. Compassion for that young person welled up inside me. I was now able to play a song and have the trauma be triggered and then be with it in the present moment from the vantage point of healing. I could give myself validation!

When Harvey taught me about Leon's traumatic brain injury, I could finally feel Leon singing with me; he'd never left me. Both Leon and Ben—along with Judy, Sandra, and Harvey—were accompanying me in An Essential Song. Harvey also gave me the chance to voice my experience to medical professionals in an effort to invoke compassion for suicidal individuals.

My present-day partner, Patty, and I had our first meeting at a free outdoor summer concert. Her adorable dog came, too! Once we became a couple, we purchased tickets to some concerts by the bands from our youth. When there, tears of gladness trickled down my cheeks. I was alive and with a loving partner in the presence of musicians who'd influenced my life in such an exceptional way. We were still here, and music would always be here for us. It had been here all along. Nothing could take it away. It would be inside me no matter what. Its availability seemed to be like that of the sky—ever-changing and ever-present. I could feel the wholeness of life in the song—the tragedy, the loss, the healing, the love. I was overcome with a sense of gratitude and a oneness with the souls who'd given me life and love. Not only had I found the song, I was singing it!

****

So, thanks for hanging out with me! Were you able to search online for the songs listed before each chapter? It'd be great if you got to read the lyrics as well as hear the instrumentation and vocalization. Words can't begin to express how much it means to me that you've stayed with me as I've tried to share some insights and provide some understanding about being suicidal. I hope I adequately answered how I worked towards living a full and meaningful life after being maimed by a suicide attempt...and that my story gives you hope.

Now I want to tell you a secret: If I were granted the magic power to expunge one minute from my life, I would not erase the one in which I drank Drano. I would keep my life as is. With all that I've lost from this tragedy has come the work I've done to accept myself...and I believe that's how I was able to find the song.

Acknowledgments

I extend my deepest gratitude and love to my soulmates:

Life Partners—

Leon Wisel (of blessed memory)

Ben Harsip (of blessed memory)

Patty Correia

Healers—

Bereavement Counselor Judy Seifert

Trauma Specialist Sandra Phinney

Physician Harvey Zarren

Special commendations to Harvey for encouraging me to write this book and for editing it with me.

Thanks to my friends at Marblehead Counseling Center (66 Clifton Avenue in Marblehead, MA 01945) for helping me establish <u>FINDING THE SONG: Restricted Fund For Suicidal Individuals</u>.